OBSERVING SCHOOLS

A Methodological Guide

Biographical details

Peter Foster taught for a number of years in comprehensive schools and sixth-form colleges. He now teaches courses on Educational Research and Research Methods in the Crewe School of Education, Manchester Metropolitan University.

Observing Schools

A Methodological Guide

Peter Foster

P·C·P
Paul Chapman
Publishing Ltd

Copyright © 1996 Peter Foster

All rights reserved

Paul Chapman Publishing Ltd
144 Liverpool Road
London
N1 1LA

British Library Cataloguing in Publication Data

Foster, Peter, 1951–
Observing Schools: a methodological guide
1. Observation (Education method) 2. Teachers – Training of
I.Title
371.1'44

ISBN 185396 266 X

Typeset by Whitelaw & Palmer Ltd, Glasgow
Printed and bound in Great Britain

A B C D E F G H   9 8 7 6

Contents

Acknowledgements

I would like to thank Martyn Hammersley for encouraging me to write this book, for commenting on earlier drafts, and, most importantly, for acting as my critical friend over the last 10 years. I am grateful also to Philip Goggin, Roger Gomm, Phil Hodkinson, Donald Mackinnon, John Robinson, John Scarth, and numerous other colleagues and students for contributing to discussions which have helped to clarify and develop my ideas on educational research.

Publisher's Acknowledgements
We are grateful to those listed below for permission to reproduce copyright material:
N. Flanders (Figure 1.1)
Open University Press (Figure 1.2)
NFER (Figure 3.3)
Professor R. Burgess (Figure 3.5)
Professor C. Pascal (Figure 3.8)
Hall, Mackay and Morgan (Figure 3.4)
Sue Cavendish, Maurice Galton, Linda Hargreaves and Wynne Harlen (Figures 3.6 and 3.7)

Introduction

Anyone who enters a school immediately begins to observe school life. As soon as a person crosses the school gates he or she sees, hears, smells, and even tastes and touches school life. Observation is a matter of collecting information about the nature of the physical and social world as it unfolds before us directly via the senses, rather than indirectly via the accounts of others. But observation is more than just this. Our minds must make sense of the data they receive. To do this we order, interpret and give meaning to incoming information. Physical objects are recognized and categorized, their category labels symbolizing their key features and qualities. Similarly, by employing our existing knowledge, conceptual schemata and theories, we recognize and give meaning to the human behaviour we witness. Usually this enables us to make sense of the world, but sometimes, particularly in unfamiliar surroundings, we may be confused and must seek further information to achieve understanding. Observation thus involves receiving data about the world through the senses, but also processing, interpreting and combining this information, in often complex ways, to form our observations – our mental images of the world and what is going on in it.

The information we collect in this way provides us with the knowledge we need in order to act in the world. So, at a very simple level, a teacher's observation of the physical environment of a school enables him or her to negotiate its corridors and classrooms, and his or her observation of the behaviour of students allows him or her to decide how to act towards them. Observational information also informs our common sense theories about the world. We act in the world on the basis of usually taken-for-granted ideas about how particular types of objects and people are likely to behave in particular circumstances, and how their behaviour will typically be affected by our own behaviour. Observing their behaviour enables us to formulate, test and modify these theories.

Some people observe school life for rather different purposes, however. What goes on within schools has been increasingly subject to the scrutiny of academic researchers, practitioner researchers, and inspectors. Their aims have also been to produce information about school life, but not the sort of information which underpins their own immediate action. The information they collect is intended to be of more general and long-term relevance. Most academic researchers, for example, see their goal as the production of generally useful knowledge about how teaching and learning occurs, and how schools are organized and run. This information is intended to inform debates about policy and practice in schools, rather than the actions of the academics themselves. Similarly, the aim of school inspections is to produce information about the quality of teaching and learning in schools which it is hoped will inform the judgement of parents and the plans of school managers and teachers. And whilst practitioner researchers often use the data they collect to inform their practice, this process is more long-term than with routine behaviour.

The observations of these researchers into school life have also been conducted in rather different ways.[1] Their methods have usually been planned and systematic, rather than haphazard and spontaneous as occurs in everyday life. Often considerable thought and preparation is put into deciding what to observe, where to observe, and how to record observations. And, generally, close attention is paid to the consistency of observational techniques, and to the systematic analysis of the data collected.

Clearly, observation is not the only method of data collection used in such enquiries. Researchers also collect valuable information by soliciting the knowledge, experiences and ideas of others through informal conversations or more formal interviews and questionnaires. They also collect information from documentary sources such as timetables, policy statements, written reports, syllabuses, school records, personal diaries, etc. But direct observation is probably the most important data collection technique used in school enquiry, and is the focus of this book.

My aim is to provide a detailed discussion of the ways in which observation is used in school research and of the issues which are raised by its use. In Chapter 1 I discuss the way observational research has developed in recent years and explore its main purposes. The key goals of different types of academic research, the aims of school-based practitioner research and the role of observation in school inspection and teacher appraisal will be considered. Chapter 2 explores the decisions that researchers must take before they conduct their observations. It looks at how researchers focus their investigations, how research projects are designed, how cases are selected for observation, how researchers gain access to settings in order to observe and how they reduce the reactivity which tends to occur as a result of the observation process. In Chapter 3 I discuss in some detail how researchers record their observations, focusing on the use of audio and video records, field notes and more structured observation schedules. Chapter 4 looks at the analysis of observational data, dealing with qualitative and quantitative data separately, but emphasizing their common goals and the considerable overlap between them. In Chapter 5 I examine the way in which the findings of observational research can be assessed, discussing the problem of evaluative criteria and applying the criteria suggested to two examples of observational research. Finally, Chapter 6 focuses on ethical issues. It considers certain key principles which have been put forward to guide research practice and examines their application to observational research in schools.

In discussing these topics I will look at a number of examples of research in schools that have employed observational methods. Often the focus of this research has been the classroom, and a significant number of the examples are of classroom research. But school research has not only been about classrooms. It has looked at other important areas of school life such as staff rooms, meetings and playgrounds, and I will draw on examples of this research too.

Another aim of the book is to bridge the gap that has developed between qualitative and quantitative methodological approaches. Educational researchers tend to divide into those who advocate the use of quantitative methods, which focus on the numerical measurement of educational phenomena, and those who favour qualitative methods, where the emphasis is on narrative description and the exploration of meaning. In my view this division is artificial and unhelpful. The investigation of educational phenomena frequently requires a combination of approaches – the rich, detailed, meaning-centred accounts produced by qualitative methods must be supplemented by information on frequency, duration and intensity produced by quantitative methods, and vice versa. Sometimes one approach is more important at a particular stage of an investigation, but more often than not both are important at some stage. Too often, in my view, researchers using qualitative methods ignore crucial quantitative dimensions, and those using quantitative methods neglect important qualitative features of the phenomena they study.

Similar issues must be addressed whichever methodological approach is adopted. All researchers interested in what goes on in schools must think about the focus of their investigations, the cases they intend to study and how these are to be selected. They must also decide how they will record their observations and maximize the accuracy of their data, and they must consider the ethical justification of their practices. So whilst there are differences in the actual procedures adopted, both qualitative and quantitative approaches face many of the same problems. And, of course, they share the same goal of producing accurate information about the nature of school life.

NOTE

1. I use the term researchers fairly loosely here to refer to anyone concerned to collect accurate information for the purpose of informing general, rather than individual, decisions about school policy and practice.

1

The Purposes of Observational Research

Observational research in schools has been conducted for a variety of purposes. The aim of this chapter is to explore these purposes and to relate them to the types of observation that are conducted. The chapter will also outline the main advantages of observation over other methods of collecting data and draw attention to some of its limitations.

ACADEMIC RESEARCH IN SCHOOLS

Thirty years ago school life and processes were rarely the focus of academic research. The academic disciplines most closely concerned with the study of education directed their attention elsewhere – psychologists to exploring the nature and development of cognitive abilities, behaviour and learning in laboratory situations, and sociologists to examining macro questions such as the social functions of education or the relationship between educational achievement and social structure. Schools were what Lacey (1970) called the 'black boxes' of the educational system. There was some study of the inputs into, and the outputs from, the boxes, but there was relatively little interest in what went on inside.

The last thirty years has seen a radical change. What goes on inside schools has increasingly come under the microscope of academic research. This trend has perhaps been most marked in the sociology of education. Here the school case studies conducted in the 1960s by Hargreaves (1967), Lacey (1970), and Lambart (1976) were influential. These researchers adopted ethnographic techniques, involving participant observation, to explore the social processes within schools which were thought to produce differential educational outcomes. Hargreaves, for example, spent a year studying a boys' secondary modern school, focusing on the relationship between differentiation produced by the school's streaming system and the increasing polarization of students' attitudes to school. He taught part time in the school and observed the behaviour of teachers and boys, both in and out of lessons, combining these data with information from questionnaires and interviews. He concluded that boys allocated to lower streams tended to develop anti-school attitudes and that this, together with the poor quality of their educational experience, tended to reduce their chances of educational success.

The development of what was termed the 'new sociology of education', and the increasing prominence of a variety of Marxist and interpretivist perspectives, also encouraged a closer study of school life. Many of the resulting studies focused on teacher perspectives and cultures, on the way teachers interpret and make sense of school life, and on the different strategies they adopt to cope with the diverse demands placed upon them. One example is Woods' (1979) study of teachers' 'survival strategies' in a secondary modern school. Like Hargreaves, Woods adopted the method of participant observation which involved him interacting with teachers and observing them at the same time. He concluded that the difficult circumstances in which the teachers worked forced them to employ classroom methods of little educational worth simply in order to get by and 'survive'.

Other researchers concentrated much more on students, examining their cultures, perspectives, interpretations and strategies. Willis (1977), for example, conducted a detailed study of the culture of a small group of working class boys in their final year of school, following them through to their first year of work. Again one of his methods was close participant observation. He found that the anti-school culture which the boys developed in school mirrored the wider working class culture that surrounded them, and was a means by which they actively resisted the alienating features of school life.

Some researchers also explored the interaction between these main participants in school life, and the processes by which order is negotiated and knowledge socially constructed and distributed. Burgess (1983), for example, again utilizing participant observation, argued that the comprehensive school he studied was an arena where differing definitions of school life were bargained over by teachers and pupils, each employing different strategies.

Lying behind many of these studies was a continued concern to describe the way educational, and resulting social, inequalities are produced, but the focus very much shifted towards a consideration of the role of school and classroom processes (see Foster, Gomm and Hammersley, 1996). In recent years academic research motivated by more directly educational, rather than sociological, questions has also concentrated on what goes on inside schools. There has been a concern, for example, to provide more accurate information about the nature of teaching and learning in order to inform educational debate more fully. This concern was the main driving force behind the Observational Research and Classroom Learning Evaluation (ORACLE) studies (Galton, Simon and Croll, 1980; Galton and Willcocks, 1983; Delamont and Galton, 1986) which sought to identify teaching styles and common interactional patterns in a representative sample of (initially primary) schools. These studies involved observers coding and counting particular behaviours in a highly systematic way in a large number of classrooms. But they also included some work using less structured approaches, similar to the participant observation studies mentioned earlier. One of their main conclusions was that teaching styles in primary schools at the time were far less 'progressive' than some commentators maintained and that most teachers adopted a range of teaching methods.

There has also been a concern to explore those features of schools which are most closely linked to differences in school effectiveness. The studies of Rutter *et al.* (1979) and Mortimore *et al.* (1988), for example, sought to relate observed differences in school organization to differences in educational outcomes between schools. Like the ORACLE studies, these projects involved systematic observation in a number of schools. A further area of interest has been the sorts of techniques teachers use in managing classrooms and teaching effectively. This has prompted a wide range of research into different aspects of classroom practice. A recent example is the Leverhulme Primary Project (Wragg, 1993) which used a number of observational methods to examine the skills of primary teachers. The researchers focused on how teachers managed their classrooms, and, more specifically, on how they used questioning and explaining in their teaching. What is perhaps most interesting about the findings of the study is, once again, the wide variation in the techniques which primary teachers use.

The fundamental purpose of this academic research in schools is the development of theoretical and empirical knowledge about what was, until recently, a relatively unexplored area. This research reveals features of school life which are frequently hidden from public view and often illuminates social processes which the participants in school life do not recognize or simply take for granted. Sometimes questions deriving from subject disciplines such as psychology or sociology are the motivating force; at other times more narrowly educational questions have provided the impetus. Either way, the main goal of this research is the description and explanation of school processes in a relatively objective and dispassionate way.

Having said this, much academic research in schools is implicitly, and sometimes explicitly, evaluative. The purpose is often to highlight what researchers consider to be inequities or examples of bad practice, in order to eliminate them or have others guard against them. Much sociological research on educational inequality, for example, is of this nature (see Foster, Gomm and Hammersley, 1996). Similarly some researchers are keen to present what they consider to be examples of good practice, so that others may emulate or learn from them. This, for example, appears to be a key purpose of some of the publications deriving from the Leverhulme Primary Project (Brown and Wragg, 1993; Wragg, 1993; Wragg and Brown, 1993).

In the academic study of school life two basic approaches to observation have developed – quantitative and qualitative – and I will examine each of these in turn.

Quantitative approaches

Quantitative approaches to observational research in schools have aimed to describe in numerical terms some of the key patterns and regularities of school life. Researchers adopting this approach try to produce accurate quantitative data on the frequency, duration, intensity and sometimes the quality of particular behaviours or patterns of interaction occurring in schools. This involves them in the careful definition of the phenomena with which they are concerned and the development of systematic methods by which frequency, duration, etc. can be measured. One of the most developed forms of quantitative observational research is systematic observation in classrooms (Croll, 1986). This involves the classification of classroom behaviours according to categories specified in an observation schedule. Perhaps the best known example is the Flanders Interaction Analysis Categories (Flanders, 1970) (see Figure 1.1). This system can be used to discover the proportion of classroom time taken up by the various teacher and student behaviours indicated in the categories. Researchers code the behaviour occurring in the classroom at three second intervals into one of ten categories and then calculate the proportion of total codings falling into particular categories. Flanders' schedule is one of a very large number that have been developed for looking at classrooms (see Simon and Boyer, 1970, 1974; Galton, 1978). These vary in focus. However, they generally record information about the physical, social or temporal context of particular behaviour or interaction patterns, and about the types of people involved so that statistical comparisons can be made between people, times, places and contexts.

As Croll (1986) points out the essential characteristic of this approach is that the purposes of observation, the categories of behaviour to be observed, and the methods by which instances of behaviour are to be allocated to categories are carefully worked out before the data collection begins. This is why this approach is often referred to as systematic or structured observation. A variety of techniques are used to record observations, but all involve some sort of pre-set, standardized observation schedule on which a record, often in the form of ticks or numbers, of the type of behaviour of interest is made.

Qualitative approaches

In contrast qualitative approaches (which are sometimes referred to as ethnographic, reflecting their origin in anthropology) have usually aimed to describe school life through detailed narrative accounts which emphasize social meanings and the cultural context of behaviour. Observational data here is often combined with information from conversations, interviews and documents to provide an in-depth picture of the perspectives and cultures of teachers and pupils as far as is possible from an insider's point of view. Burgess' (1983) study, which I referred to earlier, is a good example. Through narrative accounts of events over the course of a school year he provides a detailed picture of the way in which the norms and routines of a comprehensive school are constructed through the social interaction of teachers and pupils.

Key features of qualitative approaches are flexibility and a minimum of prestructuring. This does not mean that the observer begins data collection with no aims and no idea of what to observe, but there is a commitment to

Teacher talk	Response	1 *Accepts feeling* Accepts and clarifies an attitude or the feeling tone of a pupil in a non-threatening manner. Feelings may be positive or negative. Predicting and recalling feelings are included. 2 *Praises or encourages* Praises or encourages pupil action or behaviour. Jokes that release tension, but not at the expense of another individual; nodding head, or saying 'Um hm?' or 'go on' are included. 3 *Accepts or uses ideas of pupils* Clarifying, building, or developing ideas suggested by a pupil. Teacher extensions of pupil ideas are included but as the teacher brings more of his own ideas into play, shift to category five.
		4 *Asks questions* Asking a question about content or procedure, based on teacher ideas, with the intent that a pupil will answer.
	Initiation	5 *Lecturing* Giving facts or opinions about content or procedures; expressing *his own* ideas, giving *his own* explanation, or citing an authority other than a pupil. 6 *Giving directions* Directions, commands, or orders to which a pupil is expected to comply. 7 *Criticizing or justifying authority* Statements intended to change pupil behaviour from non-acceptable to acceptable pattern; bawling someone out; stating why the teacher is doing what he is doing; extreme self-reference.
Pupil talk	Response	8 *Pupil-talk – response* Talk by pupils in response to teacher. Teacher initiates the contact or solicits pupil statement or structures the situation. Freedom to express own ideas is limited.
	Initiation	9 *Pupil-talk – initiation* Talk by pupils which they initiate. Expressing own ideas; initiating a new topic; freedom to develop opinions and a line of thought, like asking thoughtful questions; going beyond the existing structure.
Silence		10 *Silence or confusion* Pauses, short periods of silence and periods of confusion in which communication cannot be understood by the observer.

Figure 1.1   Flanders' Interaction Analysis Categories (Flanders, 1970)

begin observation with a relatively open mind, to minimize the influence of preconceptions and to avoid imposing existing preconceived categories. The aim is to develop theoretical ideas from an analysis of the data collected so that theory is 'grounded' (Glaser and Strauss, 1967) in the data. Emerging theory is subsequently tested with more data collection in a cumulative spiral of data collection, analysis and theory development.

As one of the main aims of this type of observation is to see the social world from an insider's point of view, the researcher often participates him/herself in that world. Researchers have frequently taken on, or created, roles in the schools they have studied (most often as teachers). In this way they have been able to observe and learn the culture under study in the same way as any other new member, although hopefully with the greater detachment given by their academic role. They have typically recorded their observations, alongside data from other sources, using field notes, sometimes supplementing these with audio or video recordings.

Combining quantitative and qualitative approaches

As I explained in the introduction there has been a tendency for quantitative and qualitative approaches to be seen as competing paradigms in educational research. This is a product, to some extent, of the differing academic and epistemological roots of the two approaches. Quantitative methods developed in the main from the positivist tradition with its emphasis on the clear operationalization of concepts, the precise measurement of observable behaviour, and the examination of relationships between variables using experimental and statistical techniques. In contrast, the roots of qualitative approaches lie in anthropology and interpretivist traditions, with their emphasis on the exploration of meaning and culture.

However, in practice, much academic research combines quantitative and qualitative methods (see Bryman, 1988). Sometimes research which adopts a quantitative approach as its main method may begin with a period of qualitative observation. This may form part of the pilot work, which is used to help researchers identify the type of behaviour they wish to focus upon and develop measurement instruments, and accustom them to the research setting. In other research both quantitative and qualitative approaches can be used to shed different light on the same issue. For example, the ORACLE research on student transfer from primary to secondary schools used quantitative observations to look at teaching styles and students' adaptions to their new schools (Galton and Willcocks, 1983), and qualitative observations to explore in more depth various institutional features as well as students' experiences (Delamont and Galton, 1986). It is also quite common for research which employs a qualitative approach to utilize quantitative techniques at some stage. This may happen when the researcher requires quantitative data on particular forms of behaviour. In some of my own research (Foster, 1990a), for example, I was interested, among other things, in teacher–student interaction in multi-ethnic classes. I was concerned with whether teachers gave more of their time and attention to children from particular ethnic groups. My overall approach was qualitative, but in this case I felt the need for more quantitative data and so I used a system developed by Brophy and Good (1970a). This enabled me to count the number of different types of interaction that teachers had with students from different ethnic groups (more detail of this part of the research is contained in Foster, 1989).

PRACTITIONER RESEARCH

Observational methods have also featured prominently in much practitioner research in schools. Over the last twenty years a large number of teachers have become involved in researching their own schools and classrooms. In fact, this type of research has become institutionalized in many in-service courses and further degree work, these stressing that teachers should consciously reflect on their practice with the aim of developing and improving it.

This idea grew largely from school-based curriculum development work in the 1960s and 1970s. This work emphasized the professional autonomy of teachers and the local development of practice by individuals and groups in schools. Teachers were viewed as skilled practitioners, capable of improving their practice through continuous reflection, innovation and self-evaluation. Curriculum developers came to be seen as facilitators or collaborators – providing a basic framework of ideas and aiding in the process of critical self-reflection. An influential figure here was Lawrence Stenhouse. He argued that teachers could extend their professionalism through 'systematic self-critical enquiry' (Stenhouse, 1985; see also Stenhouse, 1975), by researching and critically examining their own practice and by testing educational theories in their own classrooms, sometimes with the assistance of colleagues or external researchers.

Stenhouse's ideas have been widely taken up. Elliott (1991), for example, advocates reflective practice or action research as a means of enhancing teachers' 'practical wisdom' – 'the practitioner's capacity for discrimination and judgement in particular, complex human situations' (p. 52). He stresses the importance of 'ethical reflection' on 'process values', seeing this as a means of resisting externally imposed technical–rational forms of teacher and curriculum development. Elliott proposes a cyclical process of action research in which teachers critically examine aspects of their current practice, introduce changes, and then monitor the effects of the changes as part of the next phase of critical examination. Figure 1.2 summarizes his action research model.

The purpose of this type of research is basically the development of practice by teachers themselves, or by teachers working in collaboration with researchers. The information produced by the research is not intended to have the same general or theoretical relevance as that produced by academic researchers, but is meant to inform the decisions made by teachers about how best to operate in the particular situations they face. As such what is suggested

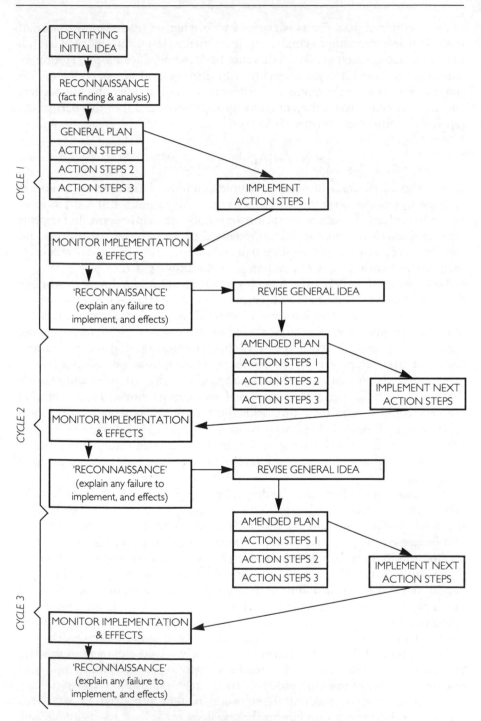

Figure 1.2 Elliott's Model of Action Research (Elliott, 1991, p. 71)

is a much more direct and immediate link between research and practice than is the case with academic research.

Observation is seen as a key data source in this type of research. It is pointed out that teachers can be participant observers in their own classrooms, and can record their observations of their own practice and its effects in the form of field notes and diaries. They can also make more detailed records of classroom action by audio or video recording their lessons. Alternatively, colleagues or research workers can observe samples of teachers' lessons and produce detailed descriptive accounts, perhaps focused on some area of concern. These accounts can then be combined with the teachers', and sometimes with the students', observations to produce detailed records of classroom action. The features of practice revealed in these data can then be examined and evaluated (possibly in collaboration with others) and any improvements thought necessary can be planned and implemented. Subsequently these can be observed and evaluated in the same way.

A number of collections of this type of research have now been published (see, for example, Nixon, 1981; Hopkins, 1985; Hustler, Cassidy and Cuff, 1986; Webb, 1990; Singh, 1994; British Educational Research Journal, 1995). One particularly interesting example is reported by Day (1981). He collaborated with teachers in the English department of a comprehensive school. Using videotapes of a sample of their lessons, the teachers worked with Day to compare their theories of how English should be taught with the reality recorded in the tapes. Using the terminology of Argyris and Schon (1976), on whose ideas the research was based, they compared their 'espoused theories' with their 'theories-in-use'.[1] In some areas the teachers found considerable incongruence and so they attempted to change their practice to bring it closer to their ideal. These changes were then subsequently observed and evaluated too. For some of the teachers the result was a considerable development of their practice.

TEACHER APPRAISAL

Another area in which observation is extremely important as a data collection technique is in teacher appraisal which has recently been introduced in schools. These schemes have their roots in concerns about educational standards and the quality of teaching which moved to the top of the educational agenda in the late 1970s, and which generated a desire to exercise greater control over teachers. Appraisal also represents an attempt on the part of some teachers and policy-makers to institutionalize the ideas of professional review and improvement which became central to the teacher-as-researcher movement. (Although some, for example Elliott (1991), see appraisal schemes as more of a bureaucratic hijacking of these ideas.)

The government included a requirement in the 1986 Education Act that teachers' performance should be regularly appraised, and over the past few years LEAs and schools have developed and implemented schemes in which all teachers' performance is appraised once every two years. A central component of the appraisal process is the observation of classroom practice, or, in the case of headteachers and other members of senior management teams, some other important aspect of their practice. Whilst resources often do not permit long periods of observation, data collected in this way provides the basis for the evaluation of the teacher's performance, following which plans are made for improvement.

A variety of approaches to observation seem to have been adopted in appraisal schemes (see Bollington, Hopkins and West, 1990; Poster and Poster, 1993). In some cases non-evaluative observations are conducted with the aim of providing a detailed factual record of practice. This is then used by the appraiser and appraisee together to develop evaluative criteria and apply them to the observed practice. The appraiser's role here is one of 'a critical friend' who facilitates self-evaluation in a similar way to that involved in action research. Another approach sometimes used is for appraiser and appraisee to negotiate evaluative criteria and the focus of assessment prior to the observation. Observations are then conducted jointly, as is the process of interpreting and evaluating performance. Here again, the relationship between appraiser and appraisee is collaborative. A third approach involves the appraiser observing and making judgements on the basis of his or her own criteria which are then given to the appraisee. Observations take the form of judgements, and the relationship between appraiser and appraisee is much more akin to that of master–apprentice. Precisely how observations are recorded and analysed is difficult to tell. Most schemes do not specify this, but suggest a variety of techniques depending on the particular aspect of the practice being observed.

THE INSPECTION OF SCHOOLS

Observation is also the main way in which school inspectors collect information in order to make their judgements about the quality of practice in schools. In recent years inspections have increased in frequency and changed in style, again largely as a result of concerns about standards of achievement and the quality of educational provision. The 1992 Education Act stipulated that all state schools must be inspected every four years by a team of inspectors recognized by the Office for Standards in Education (OFSTED).

During a school inspection judgements are made about pupils' level of achievement in relation to national norms and their potential, about pupils' 'spiritual, moral, social and cultural development', their behaviour and their attendance. Inspectors also evaluate school practices focusing on the quality of curriculum, teaching and learning, on systems for assessing, recording and reporting students' achievements and progress, and on the provision for students with special educational needs. They make judgements too about the school's efficiency in managing its resources.

Judgements are made on the basis of general criteria. In terms of teaching, for example, lessons are judged by things like the extent to which 'teachers have clear objectives', 'teachers have a secure command of the subject', and 'lessons have a suitable content' (see OFSTED, 1993a, p. 27). Judgements also relate to brief outlines of good practice in each National Curriculum subject area (see OFSTED, 1993c). But inspectors clearly rely heavily on their own notions of good practice, based on their professional experience, to decide on levels of quality.

In making their judgements inspectors use a number of sources of evidence. Perhaps the most important, especially where judgements about the quality of teaching and learning are concerned, is the direct observation of school and classroom practice. The OFSTED handbook specifies that inspectors should observe a 'sample of lessons and classes . . . [which] constitute an adequate cross-section of the work of the school' (OFSTED, 1993a, p. 10), and suggests that this should be between ten and twenty per cent of the total number of lessons during the period of the inspection (the period varies according to the size of the school).

During their observations inspectors record very little factual data. Instead they note their judgements on a set lesson proforma.[2] This proforma allows inspectors to note briefly background information, summarize lesson content and record evidence of standards of achievement, and the quality of teaching and learning. More importantly, it is used to record judgements about standards and quality in terms of a five point scale. In the case of teaching and learning this scale ranges from 1) 'Very good: many good features, some of them outstanding' to 3) 'Satisfactory: sound but unremarkable' to 5) 'Poor: many shortcomings' (OFSTED, 1993b, p. 13). The handbook concedes that sometimes it may be impossible to make judgements on all areas, but the general tenor is for judgement to be made, since lesson observations are seen as providing 'the major evidence for judgements about the quality of teaching and learning in the school as a whole' (OFSTED, 1993b, p. 12). Observations and judgements on practice outside of lessons – such as in assemblies, tutor periods and extra-curricular activities – are made on the back of this proforma. The gradings of the various members of the inspection team are collated and presented in the final inspection report in terms of percentages of observed lessons receiving particular grades. Inspectors' overall observations of strengths and weaknesses are also combined to give a composite view of a school's performance.

A number of criticisms have been expressed about this approach. First, the validity of inspectors' conclusions have been questioned because of the changes in behaviour that are precipitated by the inspection process. Anyone who has been involved in a school inspection will know that considerable efforts are made by staff to put on a good performance during the inspection period. What inspectors actually observe will therefore often be very different from what routinely occurs in a school. Second, considerable doubts have been expressed about the reliability of the evaluative procedures employed. It is suggested that often insufficient factual information is available to inspectors to enable them to make judgements, particularly on phenomena such as pupils' learning and achievement. Such phenomena are not easily observable and inspectors must therefore inevitably rely on inference from crude indicators and superficial impressions. This, combined with the largely unarticulated conceptions of good practice on which assessments are made, means that judgements are highly subjective and therefore possibly unreliable. Third, it is argued that the quantitative data produced by inspectors gives an extremely crude and over-simplified picture of the nature of the complex educational environment in a school. Commentators have pointed out that such information is of limited usefulness to practitioners or parents, other than to facilitate simplistic and possibly invalid comparisons between schools. These points have led some to conclude this whole approach to school improvement, based as it is on the fear of public humiliation and market forces, is ineffective and therefore a waste of public resources.

SCHOOL-BASED TEACHER TRAINING

Observational research in schools is also featuring more prominently in the training of new teachers. As a result of growing scepticism about the relevance of educational theory to initial practitioners, and, some would say, an increasing prejudice amongst policy-makers against educationalists in higher education, most training courses now involve students spending much more time learning about teaching in schools rather than in university departments of education. Whilst students will spend much of their time in schools actually teaching, they will also have more opportunities to observe the practice of established teachers and to research school processes. Clearly, the main purpose of this research is for them to increase their personal knowledge of practice and school organization. As such much of their observation will be informal and fairly unsystematic – the sort of everyday observation engaged in by any new entrant to a group or institution. However, students may also use some of the more systematic approaches which have been mentioned already and which will be discussed in more depth in the rest of the book.

THE ADVANTAGES AND LIMITATIONS OF OBSERVATION

These then are the main purposes of observational research in schools. Before going on to look in detail at how such research is conducted, let me briefly draw attention to the main advantages and limitations of observation as a method of collecting data.

First, observation can provide detailed information about aspects of school life which could not be produced by other methods. For example, a detailed record of the language and non-verbal communication used by teachers and students in classroom interaction could not be obtained from interviews or documents. It could only be produced by observation.

A second advantage is that it avoids relying on what participants (and others) tell us about their schools in interviews, on questionnaires and in written accounts. Those researching school life can record what they see happening in schools at first hand rather than relying on what participants say is happening. For a number of reasons participants' accounts may be inaccurate. For example, they may be shaped by the particular role the person plays in ways that make the account misleading, the information may not have been systematically recorded and may therefore contain errors, or the account may be distorted by the person's concern to present a desirable image of themselves or their school. Since observation involves the researcher noting down what he or she sees as it occurs, observational data are more likely to be accurate.

Similarly, where evaluative judgements are required it is usually inappropriate to rely on participants' views. There is often a strong motivation for participants to present favourable views of their own, or their school's, performance. Participants may also lack the expertise to make normative judgements. In these circumstances judgements based on the observations of experienced external assessors are more likely to be accurate. Moreover, observation of school practices avoids the assessment of performance against crude outcome indicators such as examination results. For student teachers a similar advantage is that observation clearly allows them to learn about the complexities of school life at first hand rather than relying on the descriptive or theoretical accounts of others.

Another advantage of observation over participants' accounts is that observers may be able to 'see' what participants cannot. Important features of school environment and processes are often taken for granted by participants and therefore may be very difficult for them to recognize, describe or evaluate. It may require the trained eye or the detached viewpoint of the observer to 'see the familiar as strange' (Delamont, 1981), and to provide the detailed description or objective assessment required. Moreover, important patterns and regularities in behaviour may only be revealed by careful, planned observation over a period of time.

A final advantage of observation is that it can give us information on those members of the school community who are unable or unwilling to take part in interviews or fill in questionnaires. Very young children, for example, are extremely difficult to interview and obviously cannot fill in complex questionnaires. Observation may be the only way of collecting information about their school experiences. It is also the case that teachers are more busy than ever before and are therefore reluctant to give time to interviews or questionnaires. Observation may be a less demanding way of collecting information from them.

At the same time, however, there are also limitations to observation as a method of collecting data. Sometimes it may be impossible to observe the behaviour or phenomenon of interest because it is inaccessible. This is obviously the case for behaviour which occurred in the past. But it may also be true where the behaviour in question deliberately avoids observation, as is often the case with deviant behaviour in schools, particularly that which occurs outside formal lessons. Sometimes, too, school personnel are extremely reluctant to allow the observation of their practice. Key gatekeepers can deny access to observers because they are apprehensive about how the observational data will be used or because they are concerned about the potential disruption the observation will cause.

A second limitation is that observation by itself may give only a partial view of behaviour. Sometimes we require further information from other sources to make sense of the data we receive. Whilst researchers looking at schools, at least in their own society, usually have considerable background knowledge of the language and culture of schools, which enables them to make sense of most behaviour they observe, there are occasions when they do not understand or fully appreciate the meanings in play. They may therefore require further information from participants about their intentions, motives, perspectives, the meaning they give to behaviour and about the cultural context from interviews, conversations and other methods, in order to understand what they observe.

This point draws attention to the fact that observations are inevitably filtered through the interpretive lens of the observer. We must remember that observations can never provide us with a direct representation of reality. Observers inevitably select what they observe and what observations they record. They also interpret what they see. The observers' existing knowledge, theories and values will inevitably influence the data they produce and the accounts and evaluations they produce. The danger is that this may introduce biases and inaccuracies into their work so that invalid, and therefore misleading, descriptions, explanations or evaluations are produced. I will discuss these problems further in Chapter 5.

Another problem is that members of the school community may, consciously or unconsciously, change the way they behave because they are being observed. If this happens, observational accounts of their behaviour will be inaccurate representations of their 'usual' behaviour, and any judgements made will be invalid assessments of normal practice. This is what is sometimes referred to as the problem of reactivity and will be discussed more fully in the next chapter.

Finally, it is important to remember that observation is a very time consuming, and therefore costly, way of collecting information. This may mean that a researcher is only able to study a restricted range of subjects or a small sample of the behaviour that is of interest. As a result, the representativeness of observations may sometimes be in doubt. In some cases interviews or questionnaires can be a more economical way of collecting detailed data which is more broadly representative.

CONCLUSION

Observational enquiry in schools has become much more common in recent years. The private nature of teaching, which Hargreaves (1982) once likened to sexual behaviour, is now open more often to public scrutiny. Moreover, the research eye has turned also to other important areas of school life – for example, to school management and decision-making, to contacts between parents and schools, and to the behaviour of teachers and pupils in staff rooms and playgrounds.

These enquiries are conducted for a variety of purposes. The aim of academic research on schools is to contribute to the development of general public knowledge of education and the way it is organized and conducted, sometimes in the hope that aspects of it can be changed or reformed. Teacher researchers have a more explicit and focused concern with reflection on, and improvement in, their own classroom practice. And those conducting observation as part of appraisal or inspection are clearly more directly concerned with evaluation and quality control.

A variety of observational methods are utilized to fit these different purposes. One distinction I have drawn is between quantitative and qualitative methods. The former are used when numerical data are required on specific behaviours or events in schools. The latter are adopted when more detailed descriptive accounts are needed which are sensitive to social context and to the meanings in play in particular situations. These approaches, and the links between them, will be explored further in the rest of the book.

NOTES

1.   These ideas were later developed in particular in Schon (1983, 1987).

2.   According to the OFSTED handbook this is intended to 'avoid distortions' and facilitate 'a systematic analysis' (OFSTED, 1993b, p. 12), though it is not clear what these phrases mean.

2

Approaching Observation

Before collecting observational data in schools researchers must think about a number of issues. First, the focus of the investigation must be established. Schools are complex institutions and the behaviour of school personnel is extremely diverse. Obviously it is impossible for an observer, or even a large team of observers, to record everything that happens in a school, or number of schools, even over a short period. And, even if this were possible, it would not be desirable. Some things which go on in schools are simply not very important or interesting. Research must therefore focus on some aspect of school life which is thought to be relevant or important. Whilst decisions about focus are usually made at the planning stage, before any observational data is collected, they are also sometimes made during the fieldwork itself, as ideas about what is important are refined and circumstances within the school(s) become clearer.

Once a focus, or at least a general area of concern, has been chosen researchers must select cases to study. Sometimes cases are specified by the purpose of the research. The purpose of a school inspection, for example, is to produce public information about a named school, and this school is therefore the case. In other studies cases are deliberately constructed in relation to the research focus. Where the focus of the research is a specific causal hypothesis the researcher may create cases which allow the hypothesis to be tested in the form of an experiment. Alternatively, naturally occurring cases may be selected which facilitate the testing of the hypothesis. More often, researchers attempt to select cases which are representative of some population about which they want information. In school research relevant populations are usually schools themselves, teachers, or pupils. But they can also be administrative units such as subject departments, or events such as appointment interviews, or specific behaviours such as pupil deviance. Researchers can rarely observe all the cases which are relevant and so they select samples.

In most studies researchers also have to negotiate access to a physical and social position from which they can observe the behaviour of interest. This usually involves getting into the schools which have been selected, and then into the various sub-settings within the school – the departments, the classrooms, the meetings, and so on – which need to be explored. It also involves adopting strategies which minimize or reduce reactivity – the effect of the researcher and the research process on what is being researched – so that, as far as possible, the subjects of the research behave in a way which is uninfluenced by the presence of an observer.

This chapter will discuss these four issues – focusing, selection strategies, gaining access and reducing reactivity.

FOCUSING

Researchers must inevitably be selective. They choose for study those areas of school life about which they, or their sponsors, feel it is important to produce information, in order to inform public debate or the decisions of policy-makers, practitioners and others. Their choices therefore usually relate closely to value concerns and current educational debates, and their aim is typically to produce information which is relevant to these.

The significance of values in providing the focus for research can be clearly seen when the impetus for research is concern about injustice or unfairness. A considerable amount of school research has been motivated by concerns about the equitable nature of school practices. Here researchers' commitments to particular views of equity have precipitated their enquiries and provided the focus for their work (see Foster, Gomm and Hammersley, 1996). Their aim has often been to discover whether or not school practice conforms to their view of equity (although these views are often not made clear). One example is a study by French and French (1984) which looked at gender inequalities in classroom talk in a sample of primary school lessons. These researchers were concerned about whether girls were disadvantaged in school by receiving less teacher attention than boys and this, together with possible explanations for the inequality they found, became the focus of their research.

Sometimes researchers motivated in these sorts of ways also attempt to intervene (usually in collaboration with practitioners) in the schools they are studying in order to change school practice in ways which will bring it more into line with their conception of equity. As a result, their interventions or actions also become the focus of their work. An example of such action research is the Girls Into Science and Technology (GIST) project based at the University of Manchester in the 1980s. This developed from a feeling that girls tended to be disadvantaged by school practices in these subjects, and therefore focused on the extent to which this occurred. But the researchers also tried to introduce practices to reduce the extent of girls' disadvantage and these also became the focus of investigation (Whyte, 1986).

The influence of values – of ideas about how things *ought* to be – can also be clearly seen in the focusing of much practitioner research. This research typically begins with some concern on the practitioner's part about the quality of some aspect of practice. He or she then focuses the research on this, collects data on it, and evaluates the practice in terms of a model of what it should be like. The practitioner then introduces changes and these become the focus of future action research. An illustration of this is reported in Hopkins (1985). A teacher was concerned about the quality of class discussions in her social studies lessons. With the aid of an outside observer she collected data on the types of questions she asked of pupils and found that, whilst many of her questions required the pupils to give opinions, very few allowed them the chance to give detailed explanations. This she felt was important in encouraging 'verbal lucidity and compositional skills'. As a result, the teacher attempted to use such questions more frequently and her future research focused on the extent to which this was effective.

A more general model of good practice underpins the evaluative research involved in school inspections. Here, as I pointed out in the last chapter, inspectors concentrate on key areas of public concern, and make judgements about these on the basis of their notions of what school practice ought to look like.

Another example of the way value concerns provide the focus of research is in the study of educational innovations. Here the aim is usually to provide information about the implementation and/or impact of a change in policy or practice in order to contribute to debates about its efficacy.[1] Consequently the implementation and impact become the focus of the research. This was the case, for example, in some of my own research which focused on how an LEA policy on multicultural education was put into practice in a comprehensive school and the effect it had on school processes (Foster, 1990a).

The focus of more academic forms of research is also influenced by value concerns, though less immediately so. This research often springs from researchers' theoretical or substantive interests, but these interests are driven by the aim of providing knowledge which will be relevant to value decisions about policy and practice. In the former case researchers may be concerned to test a particular theory or to explore the application of a theoretical idea to a new context. The theoretical questions or hypotheses therefore provide the focus of the research. One example is the considerable amount of research, conducted mainly in America, on the self-fulfilling prophecy theory – the idea that teacher expectations have an impact on students' progress. A lot of this research has focused on whether, and under what circumstances, this occurs, and the mechanisms by which any effect is produced (see Rogers, 1982 for a review).

Research foci can also derive from more substantive concerns. On the basis of his or her reading of current literature a researcher may identify an important gap in knowledge about some aspect of school life, and seek to fill it. For example, Neill (1991) found that very little research had been conducted on the different types of non-verbal communication displayed by teachers and students in classroom interaction, and therefore set about exploring the area for the first time. Alternatively a researcher may feel that the knowledge of a particular aspect of policy or practice is inadequate to inform decisions about it, and may conduct research in order to improve the situation. This feeling provided the motivation and focus for the ORACLE research (Galton, Simon and Croll, 1980) I referred to in the previous chapter. This research derived from a concern that public debate about the relative merits of different teaching styles in primary schools was based on limited information about how teachers actually taught. The researchers set out to rectify this by providing detailed descriptions of teaching practice from a wide sample of primary schools.

Research questions and foci derive therefore from value debates, and theoretical and substantive concerns. However, the stage at which a researcher's focus is clarified varies quite considerably. In more structured approaches, where the coding of observations is carried out 'live', the focus must of necessity be clearly specified and defined in advance of the fieldwork. The emphasis on quantification of specific behaviours, often by a team of observers working in different schools, requires that the behaviours of concern are defined clearly and that standardized procedures are adopted. Similarly, in school inspections the foci of observations, although very general, are established before inspectors go into schools to try to ensure that a consistent approach is adopted.

In contrast, with less structured approaches the initial focus is often rather vague and ill-defined. Research questions may be often broad and general, and researchers usually aim to be flexible and responsive to the ideas and issues which emerge during the course of data collection. Often, therefore, the focus of initial observations is wide and the researcher is concerned, like any new member of a group or institution, to obtain a broad overview and basic information. At this stage the researcher will probably record, in a fairly unselective way, any observations which appear to be potentially relevant or interesting. As the research progresses, however, more specific research questions and hypotheses usually emerge from the examination and analysis of initial data. These then provide the focus for future data collection. This gradual refinement of research questions is sometimes referred to as 'progressive focusing'. In much practitioner and action research there is also a commitment to flexibility of focus. Although the initial focus of this type of research is on some concern about practice, these concerns often change during the process of data collection and reflection.

Another distinction which is sometimes important to make is between the phenomenon which is the focus of the research and the behaviour that is the focus of observation. Researchers are often concerned with types of phenomena which are not observable in a direct or straightforward way – things like attitudes, qualities, mental processes or generalized behavioural categories. As a result they often employ indicators of the phenomenon; that is more easily observable behaviour which signifies the existence of the phenomenon of concern. For example, French and French (1984), in the study I have just referred to, used the number of turns at talk in a class discussion as an indicator of the distribution of teacher attention between boys and girls in the classroom. Similarly, in a study of preschool education (Pascal, Bertram and Ramsden, 1994), which I will discuss further in the next chapter, researchers used a number of aspects of children's behaviour, such as their facial expressions and posture, body movements, language, and the duration of their activities, as indicators of their level of involvement in activities and hence of the quality of their learning experiences. Thus, whilst the focus of research may be on general categories of phenomena, the actual observation and recording may be concerned with behavioural indicators.

SELECTION STRATEGIES

1. Selecting cases

The types of case which researchers select for study are determined by the focus of their investigations. Where their focus is the general nature or quality of what goes on in schools, schools are, of course, the cases they will select. Where the focus is on the behaviour of teachers or pupils, then teachers or pupils will be the cases. Similarly, if the focus is on particular administrative units (subject departments, for example), or areas (playgrounds, for example), or events (lessons, for example) then these will be the cases.

The strategies used to select cases depend on the aims of the investigation. A common aim is to produce descriptive information about a particular population of cases – about schools, teachers, departments, lessons or whatever – and an attempt is made to select a sample of cases which is representative in key respects of the target population. Where an accurate list of the population is available (sometimes referred to as a sampling frame) then this selection can be done by random methods. As long as there is no systematic pattern in the list, the researcher can simply select cases at regular intervals from the list according to the number required in the sample. Alternatively, they can number the cases in the population and use a list of random numbers to select the cases needed.[2] So, for example, a researcher interested in selecting a representative sample of primary teachers from within an LEA might select at random from a list of primary teachers supplied by the LEA. Or a researcher concerned to study a representative sample of lessons in a school might select at random from all the lessons on the timetable over a particular period.

The advantage of random sampling is that it eliminates any systematic bias that might occur in the selection of cases. This maximizes the chances that the sample will have similar characteristics to the population as a whole. In practice, of course, this may not be the case because chance can result in samples which differ considerably from the population. This is why, if they can, researchers check the representativeness of their samples by comparing their characteristics with known characteristics of the population. In addition, where random selection has been employed, it may be possible to calculate the probability of the sample being representative (Bryman and Cramer, 1990).

Sometimes this type of sampling can involve a number of stages or levels. When pure random sampling would result in a widely spread selection of cases, which would be inconvenient and costly to access, then researchers may select cases randomly from naturally occurring clusters. For example, if a researcher wanted to study a sample of secondary school teachers in a region he or she might first select a random sample of schools from the region, and then choose a random sample of teachers from within those schools.

Another strategy which is sometimes adopted for pragmatic reasons is quota sampling.[3] Here researchers select cases which have a similar range of characteristics to the known characteristics of the population. For instance, a researcher might select a number of schools for study which reflect the key characteristics – in terms of say size, catchment area, intake, and so on – of the population of schools he or she is interested in. Or a researcher might choose a sample of teachers which has a similar profile of characteristics – in terms of say age, gender, length of experience – to the population of teachers that is the focus. Such a strategy is an attempt to achieve a degree of representativeness without the use of random sampling.

More often, school research concentrates on a single case, or on a small number of cases. Here the aim is to study the case(s) in depth. Researchers adopting qualitative or ethnographic approaches often adopt this strategy. In this type of research an attempt is sometimes made to select a typical case, or, as with the quota sampling I have just referred to, to select cases which have characteristics similar to those of the wider population. Hargreaves (1986), for example, in a study of policy and practice in middle schools selected two case study schools which he felt were typical in some respects of well established middle schools in England, although he concedes that in terms of their organizational characteristics it was impossible to assess their typicality, since such information on the population of middle schools was not available.

The limitation of this strategy is, of course, that a single case, or small number of cases, may not be representative of the wider population in the relevant respects. Whether this is so depends in part on how heterogeneous the population is in these respects. Generally one must be cautious in making general claims about the features of a wider population on the basis of in-depth studies of a small number of cases. This is especially true where the cases are selected on a purely pragmatic basis, as often happens given resource constraints and access difficulties. Sometimes cases are selected because they are close to the researcher's work base or because the researcher has some personal contact which facilitates access. Researchers often feel that such choices are justified because the knowledge of these cases in themselves will be valuable. They concede that the particular case(s) they have studied may be untypical, but argue that their findings produce important information or generate interesting ideas and questions which can be followed up by other researchers or utilized by practitioners.

Where the aim of the investigation is the testing of a theory or causal relationship different selection strategies are usually adopted. One approach is the deliberate construction of cases in an experimental design. In its pure form an experiment involves testing the relationship between two variables by deliberately manipulating one (the independent variable) and monitoring any changes in another (the dependent variable) whilst controlling all other relevant variables. This can involve the random allocation of subjects to different treatment groups and the standardization of conditions such that the only difference in the treatment of the two groups is in terms of the independent variable. But for practical and ethical reasons such control is not often possible in school research. Comparisons are therefore usually made between similar groups, in similar conditions, which are deliberately treated differently. These are sometimes referred to as quasi-experiments (Campbell and Stanley, 1963).

An example is a study conducted by Wheldall and Olds (1987) of the effects of mixed-sex seating on the classroom behaviour of pupils in a junior school. The researchers selected two mixed ability classes with pupils of similar ages and with a similar balance of sexes. Normally in one class the pupils sat next to a member of the same sex and in the other to a member of the opposite sex. For a two week period this was reversed. The researchers observed and recorded the proportion of lesson time that pupils in each class were 'on-task' before, during and after the intervention period. Here the independent variable was mixed- or same-sex seating and the dependent variable was the level of on-task behaviour amongst the pupils. By making comparisons between the two classes, and between the same class before, during and after the intervention, the researchers were able to test their hypothesis that mixed-sex seating would result in a higher level of on-task behaviour. The researchers found that in all the situations of mixed-sex seating pupils spent more lesson time on-task.

Comparisons are also sometimes made between similar groups in similar conditions whose treatment differs naturally. An interesting example is Brophy and Good's (1970b) study of the effects of teachers' expectations on classroom interaction. These researchers observed and compared the nature of teacher interaction with groups of pupils about which the teachers had high or low academic expectations. Thus they examined the effect of two naturally occurring conditions (high or low teacher expectations) – which defined the cases – on the teachers' actions in the classroom. Their findings were complex, but revealed that in certain crucial respects the teachers favoured pupils of whom they had high expectations.

These comparison strategies often underpin the study of educational innovations or action research as well. Sometimes these studies involve the comparison of two groups – a group exposed to the innovation and a similar group who are not – in order to assess the impact of the change. On other occasions comparisons are made of the same group before, during and after the innovation, again to examine whether the change has had the desired effect.

Another selection strategy which is sometimes adopted with the aim of testing a theory is the study of a critical case. Here a case is chosen which is most or least likely to fulfil a particular theoretical expectation, and the aim is to see whether or not the case conforms to the expectation. An example is Hargreaves' (1981) study of 'contrastive rhetoric and extremist talk' in the curriculum development meetings of one of the middle schools he studied.

Hargreaves argues that this school provided a critical case for the testing of the Marxist derived theory that teachers' thinking is hegemonically determined – in other words that it is hostile to radical educational and social ideas which might threaten the existing capitalist order. He claims that the school, because it was new, with innovative, young, forward-thinking staff, was a place where one might least expect teachers' thinking to be hostile to such ideas. The fact that he found considerable conservatism amongst the teachers disconfirmed this expectation, and suggested that hostility was probably quite widespread.

Sometimes this strategy is broadened to the selection of several cases which test a number of expectations deriving from a theory. This is often referred to as theoretical sampling (Glaser and Strauss, 1967). Hammersley and Scarth's (1986) research on the influence of modes of assessment on the nature of teaching in secondary schools is a useful illustration of this. They were concerned to test the theory that examination-based forms of assessment tended to lead to more traditional, didactic forms of teaching. They therefore selected a variety of courses for study which had different modes of assessment (their cases) – on some courses assessment was exam based, on others it involved various degrees of course work.The teaching on these courses was compared in terms of the degree of participation of teacher and pupils in public classroom talk, these being seen as indicators of levels of didacticism in teaching. Moreover, the researchers also compared the nature of teaching on courses with similar assessment modes to see if there were significant differences. Thus Hammersley and Scarth deliberately selected cases in order to explore the extent to which differences in teaching were produced by differences in the mode of assessment.

This strategy, or aspects of it, has sometimes been implicit in other school research. For example, the research conducted by Rutter et al. (1979) selected 12 secondary schools in inner London for study. The aim was to discover whether the schools differed in effectiveness and, if so, then which of their internal features contributed to this. The researchers argue that one advantage of the 12 schools selected was that they were similar in terms of catchment area and intake, and this made it more likely that any difference between them in educational outcomes was a product of internal school factors.

2. Selection within cases

Once cases have been selected it is often necessary to further select within the case itself. For example, where a school is chosen for an in-depth study researchers usually have to select for observation from the large amount of behaviour relevant to their focus which occurs in the school. Similarly, where a number of teachers or pupils are chosen as cases researchers must usually choose for observation examples of their behaviour from the range which is relevant. And even when the cases chosen are relatively narrow in scope, such as specific lessons, selection is often required to make observation more manageable. In one sense selection in these situations can be seen as a further extension (to a lower level) of the multi level sampling I mentioned in the previous section. What happens is that the cases themselves become the populations from which sub-cases are chosen.

Again, one strategy which is sometimes used to select within cases is random sampling. For example, a researcher might select for observation a random sample of a teacher's lessons, or of pupils from within a class, or of meetings in a school. Another example is the time (or point) sampling which is sometimes used in more structured forms of observation. Here the researcher records the behaviour occurring in the situation he or she is interested in at regular points in time (or records the behaviour which occurs in a particular, brief time period). This was the technique used in the ORACLE project (Galton, Simon and Croll, 1980), where teacher and student behaviour were each observed at 25 second intervals. The assumption here is that the resulting sample is random and therefore representative of the whole period of observation. This may be quite likely, but it is not necessarily the case. Sometimes the patterning of behaviour over time can result in unrepresentative samples. Unfortunately, this is rarely checked by researchers.

Another selection strategy is the quota sampling I discussed in the previous section. Within a school case study, for example, a researcher might select a sample of teachers or pupils who fit the known characteristics of the particular population in the school. And he or she could adopt similar techniques with the selection of times, places, and events. The aim again is to select a sample which contains a range of examples similar to those found in the population and which is therefore more likely to be representative.

Theoretical sampling is also possible within cases. However, here it can have a slightly different function from that outlined earlier. In ethnographic case studies data collection and analysis usually proceed hand in hand, and theoretical sampling is sometimes used to refine an emerging descriptive model. All description involves the development of conceptual categories in order to summarize the key features of the phenomena of concern and theoretical sampling can assist this process. Glaser and Strauss (1967), who recommend this strategy, suggest that researchers select instances of the behaviour they are interested in to clarify the range and nature of the category system they are using to describe the behaviour. This selection can occur at the data collection stage or during analysis (see Chapter 4) where instances are selected from data already collected. The idea here is that researchers should maximize the differences between instances in order to establish the range of behaviour to which a particular category system (or category within a system) can apply. They can also minimize the difference between instances in order to establish the key defining characteristics of particular categories. Essentially, Glaser and Strauss recommend the constant comparison of selected instances to clarify a descriptive model, and suggest that this approach is adopted until categories are 'saturated', that is until nothing new is being learned about the categories.

An example will perhaps clarify these ideas. Woods (1979) claimed that much of the behaviour of the teachers he observed in a secondary modern school could be described as 'survival strategies', and that there were 8 types of such strategy – domination, negotiation, socialization, fraternization, absence or removal, ritual and routine, occupational therapy, and morale-boosting. Woods, as with many researchers who use ethnographic methods, does not give much information about the way he developed this category system to describe teachers' behaviour, but we can speculate on how he might have used Glaser and Strauss' suggestions. First, particularly in the early stages of his research, he could have maximized the differences between instances by selecting a wide variety of teachers' behaviour to clarify what range of behaviours could legitimately be categorized as survival strategies. Second, as his research progressed he might have minimized the differences between instances by selecting for more detailed scrutiny those categorized as survival strategies or as particular types of survival strategy. This would have enabled him to clarify the key features of these particular categories. This method of selecting and comparing instances of teacher behaviour and, more specifically, of teacher behaviour categorized in different ways would have facilitated the development of Woods' descriptive model.

Theoretical sampling can also be used within cases to test emerging causal hypotheses in the way I outlined earlier. As with the selection of critical cases the researcher can choose instances which are most or least likely to fulfil a particular theoretical expectation. For example, he or she might be interested in the relationship between teachers' survival strategies and the number of students with behavioural problems in a class. More specifically he or she might put forward the hypothesis that the adoption of survival strategies was more likely the higher the number of such students in a class. In order to test this hypothesis he or she could again maximize the differences between observational categories – by looking at teaching in classes with high and low numbers of students with behavioural problems – and also minimize the differences by comparing teaching in classes with similar numbers of such students. By comparing instances in this way the researcher could clarify the link between these two variables.

Having said all this about representative and theoretical sampling it is important to recognize the practical limitations on selection strategies within case studies. Accurate sampling frames are often not available, data analysis is frequently rushed and incomplete, and access to particular times, places or events may be limited or difficult to obtain. In fact pragmatic considerations are usually paramount. What a researcher actually selects to observe is often very much dependent on the opportunities that arise, the role that he or she plays and the relationships that are developed with teachers, pupils and others. Often observation depends on the co-operation of these subjects and of key 'gatekeepers' who control access to important parts of the setting (of which more in a moment). Researchers sometimes simply have to concentrate their observations on those situations to which they can gain access.

One selection strategy which is sometimes used when access to some subjects or situations is proving difficult is 'snowball sampling'. Here one subject passes the researcher on to another, vouching for him or her and acting as a sponsor. The advantage is that sponsorship encourages co-operation and facilitates access, but, of course, the resulting sample may be unrepresentative.

GAINING ACCESS

Clearly in order to observe what happens in a school researchers have to gain physical access to it and to its relevant sub-settings – the departments, classrooms, meetings and so on. In the case of school inspections access rights are specified by law, and although inspectors must give notice to a school of their intention to inspect and indicate the time they will spend in the school, they do not require the school's permission to conduct their inquiries. With academic research, however, there are no rights of access. Schools can refuse or place restrictions on access, and gaining permission to conduct observational research often involves complex and sometimes protracted negotiations (see for example Walford, 1991). Indeed, there is evidence that such negotiations are less likely to be successful nowadays (Troman, 1996). Practitioner researchers may also face problems. Although they are usually already in the school as members of staff, they may need to obtain permission to conduct their research from those in positions of authority in the school and from colleagues who they hope to involve.

Different types of research require different forms of access. Sometimes, particularly on projects using more structured methods, access is required for short periods to a relatively large number of schools for several different observers. In smaller scale projects, frequently employing less structured methods, often a lone researcher is concerned to gain access to a single or small number of schools for a relatively long period. At the beginning of this sort of research the focus may be unclear and the researcher may be unsure which sub-settings within the school he or she is interested in. Consequently, access remains an issue throughout data collection as entry into various sub-settings has to be negotiated, and sometimes renegotiated, as the research progresses. In the case of practitioner research physical access to the school is not normally the issue. What is usually required here is permission for the teacher to engage in an activity which is not always seen as part of his or her role, though sometimes access to the classrooms of others might be needed.

Gaining access or permission to do research usually requires negotiation with a number of gatekeepers, sometimes at different levels of the school hierarchy. Gatekeepers, who may also be the subjects of the research, can grant or withhold permission to conduct research in their particular sphere of authority. In gaining access to the school itself the researcher would probably have to negotiate with LEA officers (if the school was LEA maintained), governors, and the headteacher, and then, in order to gain access to sub-settings within the school, he or she would have to approach heads of department, teachers and perhaps pupils and parents too. This often involves time consuming discussions, although the process can sometimes prove a useful source of information on the political structure of the school and the perspectives of key personnel.

Gatekeepers are often concerned to protect their own interests, and the interests of the school or sub-group, from any threat or disruption posed by the research. They may therefore refuse access altogether, place limitations on the type of research which can be done, or try to manage the impression of the school or group that the researcher receives and documents. The latter may involve presenting the school, groups or individuals to the researcher in a particular way, restricting or facilitating access to particular areas, times or events, and/or influencing or constraining what the researcher can publish. Of course, where the purpose of the research is evaluation which is to be made public, as it is with school inspections, then considerable efforts may be made to manipulate the picture of the school received by the researchers, something which raises questions about the validity of findings in these studies. Gatekeepers may also try to use the research to serve their own purposes. It is not uncommon, for example, for headteachers to agree to access but then expect researchers to supply them with information about the performance of more junior members of staff.

One of the factors which influences the response of gatekeepers to access requests is their preconceptions of research and researchers. These derive from any previous experience of research they have had, and from the way research is presented to them by others or by the media. Sometimes their conceptions of research and researchers may be negative; they may think research is irrelevant or divorced from important concerns, or that researchers are untrustworthy and likely to misrepresent what they see; in which case they are unlikely to grant access. On the other hand, their view may be more positive and the researcher may be welcomed and given considerable assistance. More commonly, the conceptions of gatekeepers consist of a mixture of positive attitudes and scepticism, trust and suspicion.

In negotiating access, researchers try to influence the conceptions gatekeepers have of their research. They adopt a number of strategies. Sometimes they simply explain fully the purposes and nature of the research, and the methods to be employed, in the hope that gatekeepers will be sufficiently interested and willing to allow the research to go ahead. This was the approach adopted by Stenhouse and his team who conducted research on library use in school sixth forms (Stenhouse 1984). They wrote to headteachers explaining the aims of their project and the research methods they planned to use, and offered to visit the school to discuss the research at greater length. Most of the schools approached agreed to take part in the research.

On occasions, however, the account of the research given may be selective or involve an element of deception. This is often because the researcher feels that access will be denied, or subjects will behave differently, if he or she presents a completely accurate account. Part of my own research in a multi-ethnic school (Foster, 1990a) was concerned with whether teachers gave more attention to students from certain ethnic groups. When negotiating access to classrooms for this part of the research, I did not tell the teachers this was specifically what I was interested in because I thought that if I did they would make a conscious effort to distribute their attention equally. I kept my explanation deliberately vague and said I wanted to observe teaching methods and student behaviour.[4]

Researchers are also concerned to influence how gatekeepers see them as people. They therefore use, consciously or unconsciously, many self-presentation techniques to convey an impression of themselves which will maximize their chances of gaining access. They dress and conduct themselves in ways which will give the impression that they will 'fit in' and that their presence is unlikely to cause offence, disruption or harm to subjects, and that they can be trusted. Delamont, for example, reflecting on her research in a Scottish girls' public school in the 1960s, describes how she 'always wore a conservative outfit and real leather gloves' when meeting headteachers. On the other hand, she wished to give a slightly different impression to the students so wore a dress of 'mini-length to show the pupils I knew what the fashion was' (Delamont, 1984, p. 25).

Another technique used when negotiating access is to offer inducements to gatekeepers. Researchers may, for instance, emphasize the potential knowledge gains to the educational community as a whole or to the school itself in comparison to the small amount of time or disruption that the research will require. In the case of practitioner research they may argue that the research will facilitate the development of their own and their colleagues' professional effectiveness. More traditional researchers sometimes offer services in return for access and enter into bargains with gatekeepers. For example, a number of researchers who have conducted ethnographic case studies of schools have taken on a part-time teaching load in part to facilitate access (see, for example, Hargreaves, 1967; Lacey, 1970; Burgess, 1983), and in my research (Foster, 1990a) I offered to act as a 'consultant' to the school which involved encouraging teachers to reflect on and improve aspects of their practice.

Researchers will also usually offer to protect the interests of subjects by guaranteeing the confidentiality of data, using pseudonyms in publications, and/or stressing their commitment to established ethical principles (see Chapter 6). Sometimes gatekeepers are offered some control over the research – perhaps the opportunity to scrutinize, and maybe veto, plans and research techniques, or to have some say in the use of data or the publication of a final report. Walford and Miller (1991), for example, who studied Kinghurst, a new City Technology College, offered the headteacher the opportunity to write an unedited 15,000-word section of the planned book to encourage her to give them access (see Walford, 1991 for a discussion). Of course, in most practitioner and action research collaboration between researchers and subjects is seen as central to the research process. (Indeed the subject may be the researcher.) It is suggested by some that not only does this facilitate access, but it also respects more fully the rights of subjects to be consulted and involved, and means that the research is more likely to address their concerns and produce information that they will find useful.

Another strategy sometimes used in gaining access, especially in ethnographic research, is to utilize the assistance of a sponsor. This is generally a relatively well-established figure within the school with whom the researcher has some existing personal contact. This person can reassure others in the school about the identity of the researcher and sometimes about the purposes of the research. In my research (Foster, 1990a), for example, I relied to some extent on the assistance of a head of department whom I knew from meetings when I had been in a similar position in a nearby school. By speaking favourably of me and the research she was very influential in my gaining access to the school and to her particular department. She also acted as a useful initial guide to the school introducing me to its structure and organization, and to key personnel. In fact, throughout the research she was a key informant, providing a valuable source of data on events which I was unable to observe myself. The only drawback was that my close association with her perhaps made those who were not in tune with her views less likely to accept me. For example, two teachers who frequently disagreed with her opinions in staff meetings were very reluctant to become involved with my research, although it is difficult to know how much this was due to my link with her.

A more controversial strategy sometimes used to gain access is to conduct research secretly. Here access to the school, or parts of it, is obtained by the researcher secretly taking on an established role or, more likely, using his or her existing role to conduct research secretly. No formal permission to do the research is requested. The researcher simply becomes, or already is, a participant member of the school and uses this position to observe the behaviour of other participants. Covert research is most likely to be used where there is a strong possibility that access or permission to do the research will not be gained by more open methods or when reactivity is likely to be a problem if the research is conducted openly.

I know of no examples in school research of outside researchers secretly posing as teachers or pupils in order to conduct their research (the latter would, of course, be rather difficult given the age of most researchers) though there are examples of this kind of research in other areas (see, for example, Festinger, Riecken and Schachter, 1956; Patrick, 1973; Rosenhan, 1982). What is more common in school research is for researchers to use their existing practitioner roles to conduct research (in fact, the idea of practitioner research encourages this), and that this research is conducted covertly, for at least some of the time or with some of the subjects. A number of school case studies have been conducted by teachers, or by teachers who later move more formally into the academic community and become researchers. It is often difficult to know to what extent this type of research is conducted secretly. Researchers are rarely clear about who was informed about their research and whose permission was sought. I suspect in many cases that, although certain people are informed and asked about the research, many others are unaware that the teacher is also conducting a piece of research. This particularly applies to pupils who are rarely consulted and often seen as 'captive' subjects of research.[5]

Sometimes part of a research project is conducted secretly. Hammersley (1980), for example, negotiated access to a school to conduct research on the classroom interaction of teachers and students, but found that the conversations he heard between teachers in the staff room were an interesting source of data. Indeed, his research focus shifted somewhat to the content of these conversations and their function in developing teachers' typifications of students and maintaining a particular teacher culture. He explains (Hammersley, 1984, 1990a) that, although the teachers in the school knew he was a researcher, he did not explicitly draw their attention to the fact that he was collecting data in the staff room, and he recorded the conversations surreptitiously, sometimes jotting them down on the edges of a newspaper. He felt that had he been completely open about this part of his research the teachers would probably have refused him permission to carry on with any of his research, or they would have behaved very differently in the staff room. I think many researchers, although they may be reluctant to admit it, have adopted similar practices at some stage in their research. This discussion obviously raises questions about what we mean by secrecy and deception in school research, and whether or to what extent they are justified. I will return to these questions in Chapter 6.

REDUCING REACTIVITY

Researchers are not only interested in gaining physical access to schools and relevant areas within schools, they are also concerned with observing the behaviour which naturally occurs in these settings. In other words, they desire access to behaviour which has been influenced as little as possible by the researcher's presence or the research process. The latter form of reactivity is, of course, eliminated in covert research because subjects are not aware they are being studied. The former is not, however, because the researcher in his or her participant role may have an influence on behaviour. The extent and form of this reactivity clearly depends on the nature of the participant role being played in the particular situation being observed, and on the way subjects interpret and respond to the behaviour of the participant observer.

In a small number of research projects there is an attempt to eliminate both forms of reactivity by the researcher observing covertly and not interacting at all with subjects. Research has sometimes been conducted from vantage points which conceal the observer, or at least result in minimum contact. This was the case in the early stages of a study by Corsaro (1981) which examined children's behaviour on entry to a nursery school. He utilized a pre-existing observation area of the school which was equipped with a one-way window. He was able to observe the children without them being aware of his presence or that they were being observed. (He later moved into the main body of the school and observed whilst participating with the children in their activities). Another example is a study of children's playground aggression and playfighting conducted by Serbin (reported in Pellegrini, 1991) in which children's behaviour was observed with binoculars from an adjacent building. Again the children were apparently unaware that they were being observed.[6]

Hidden observation is rarely possible in school research. Where it is, the elimination of the reactivity which stems from the physical presence of the researcher can be a distinct advantage, particularly where subjects, such as very young children, are likely to behave differently when an unfamiliar person is around. Another advantage is that the observer does not get drawn into interaction, which again can often happen with young children, being left free to concentrate on data recording, and possibly even to discuss data with another observer whilst collecting it.

However, this approach does have limitations. There are obvious restrictions on what can be observed. Also, the researcher may not be able to collect supporting data by asking the subjects questions. As a result, he or she may fail to appreciate the perspectives of the subjects and to understand the social meanings which underpin their interaction. As I pointed out in Chapter 1, these additional sources of data may be essential if the researcher is to make sense of his or her observations. This is one reason why this role is most often used in more structured observation where the researcher is interested mainly in categorizing instances of predefined behaviour.

Researchers who conduct their observations more openly usually use a number of techniques to become unobtrusive in the setting and hence minimize reactivity. They often select their own physical location and the positioning of any recording equipment they are using very carefully in order to minimize reactivity. They also take care to dress and behave in ways which will allow them to blend into the setting – the aim being to reduce the extent to which subjects are conscious of their presence and of their observation. King (1984), for example, during his research in infant school classrooms, used his height to distance himself (literally) from the children and tried to avoid eye contact with them. He also at one stage used the 'Wendy House' as a 'convenient "hide"'.

Researchers using ethnographic methods often spend considerable periods of time in the field so that subjects become accustomed to their presence. They also make great efforts to build relationships of trust with subjects in order to facilitate access and reduce reactivity. As with discussions with gatekeepers, what is involved here is the negotiation of the researcher's identity with subjects. The researcher wishes to be seen as a certain type of person – usually as someone who is non-judgemental, empathetic, and understanding – and will try to influence, sometimes consciously, but often unconsciously, the way he or she is perceived by controlling or manipulating the information that subjects receive. Subjects (like gatekeepers) will have certain preconceptions and developing conceptions of the researcher, both as a person and as a researcher. The researcher tries to build on or change these initial conceptions using similar techniques of impression management to the ones I discussed earlier.

For example, he or she will dress in ways which display his or her identification with the subjects rather than with potentially threatening groups. In my own research (Foster, 1990a), for example, I usually dressed in the casual manner of many of the classroom teachers, avoiding the formality of dress which was associated with 'senior management' or inspectors.

Researchers also sometimes present their existing experience, skills and knowledge in ways which facilitate a non-threatening identity. Again, in my own research I frequently made use of my experience of teaching in a nearby school to convey the impression that I was knowledgeable about, and sympathetic to, the teachers' concerns – in a sense that I was one of them – rather than some sort of expert or critic. On reflection I also, generally unconsciously, presented myself as, for want of a better phrase, an ordinary, decent type of person – someone who was honest, approachable, friendly, sensitive and understanding. I did this by engaging in ordinary, everyday, sociable conversations, openly discussing aspects of my past and present life and exchanging day-to-day information. This type of self-presentation is crucial in gaining the acceptance and trust of subjects. Also important, of course, is how the researcher actually behaves. He or she has to demonstrate his or her trustworthiness, openness, reliability and so on, since behaviour provides subjects with direct evidence of the researcher's attributes. Indeed, subjects may sometimes actually test the researcher out in these respects.

On some occasions the researcher may be more consciously selective in the self they present to subjects. He or she may play down or conceal certain aspects by, for example, disguising or failing to reveal his or her personal views or ideological commitments. It would have been very difficult, for example, for Hammersley (1980) to continue with his research had he revealed his disagreement with the views on race which teachers expressed in staff room conversations in the school he studied. On occasions too it may be necessary for the researcher to deliberately construct aspects of his or her identity in order to facilitate an appropriate impression. This is most likely where the researcher's existing characteristics are likely to result in suspicion or hostility from subjects. Research on deviant students, for example, has often required researchers to manipulate aspects of their identity in these sorts of ways. Again these strategies raise ethical questions which I will explore in Chapter 6.

Of course, there are limits to the identities that researchers can negotiate with subjects. Ascribed characteristics such as age, gender and race, and the limitations of the researcher's knowledge and skills, restrict the sort of person he or she can become and the sort of relationship that can be developed with subjects. As a middle-aged male I would obviously find it difficult to develop close peer-type relationships with pupils or to be seen as non-threatening by pupils who were engaged in delinquent activities. On the other hand I would find it easier to cultivate relationships with teachers or to be seen as a responsible, professional researcher by school governors. In saying this, I do not mean to imply that the researcher must be of the same age, gender or race as his or her subjects. It is simply that sometimes these characteristics aid in the construction of certain identities and therefore facilitate relationships with some subjects rather than with others.

Another strategy which is sometimes adopted in negotiating a non-threatening identity is for the researcher to take on, or utilize, an existing participant role in the school. As I have already explained, in a number of school case studies researchers have worked as teachers whilst also acting as researchers. As well as facilitating access, working alongside teachers helps to show that the researcher is empathetic and trustworthy. As a result some teachers at least (and possibly some pupils too) are less likely to put on a front and more likely to be honest and open with the researcher. Indeed, it may be that, because the researcher is a participant, teachers and pupils forget that he or she is doing research, and thus behave more naturally. At times like this it might be said that the research becomes covert, although it is difficult to tell when this happens.

The other main advantage of taking on, or using, an existing role is that the researcher is better able to see the social world from the point of view of his or her subjects. As a real member of the school or group he or she knows or has to learn the culture of the groups or institution because he or she has to operate in it. The researcher gains access to inside information and is more likely to appreciate the subjects' perspectives and the meanings which underpin their behaviour.

However, taking on, or using, an existing participant role does have some limitations. Access to certain people and areas of the school will be restricted by the rules and norms which apply to the participant role. For example, a researcher who takes on the role of classroom teacher is likely to find it more difficult to access the world of pupils, or to gain access to senior staff meetings. Having a participant identity means the researcher will also be seen by subjects as having particular characteristics, ideas and commitments. This may increase, or produce a different form of, reactivity on the part of some subjects. For instance, teachers observed by one of their colleagues may be more concerned to make what they feel is a good impression than if they were observed by an external non-participant researcher. And pupils observed by a person they see as a teacher will adjust their behaviour accordingly.

Playing an established role can also be very time consuming and mean that little time is available for recording data. This means that the researcher must put greater reliance on memory to record his or her observations, with the consequent greater risk of error or distortion. It can sometimes be stressful too, particularly for an external researcher. He or she will want to be seen to perform the role competently (or at least not incompetently), but this may be difficult, particularly if he or she lacks the appropriate skills or experience. Performing the teaching role, for example, is not easy in some schools, particularly in the first few months when a teacher's reputation must be established. Unless the researcher carries off the role competently, or at least to a level of incompetence characteristic of other new teachers, he or she is unlikely to gain the confidence and trust of other teachers and maybe also of pupils. There is also the stress which occurs when the expectations of the participant role are in conflict with those of the research role, something which gives rise to some difficult ethical dilemmas.

An associated problem is what is sometimes termed 'going native'. In playing an existing role the researcher may identify too closely with his or her subjects. He or she may lose, or never develop, a sense of detachment and therefore present an over-sympathetic view of subjects. This is a particularly difficult problem for practitioner researchers who sometimes find it very difficult to take a detached or critical view of their own practice or that of their colleagues. This problem is not confined to situations where the researcher plays an existing role,[7] but it becomes more likely the more involved the researcher is with his or her subjects.

For these reasons some researchers avoid taking on existing roles in the school they are studying, preferring to emphasize their role as researcher. Typically the researcher is 'the person writing a book about . . .' or 'the person investigating . . .'. Woods (1979), for example, in his study of a secondary school, thought of himself as an 'involved' rather than a participant observer. He deliberately did not take an existing role in the school, although he did occasionally help out with lesson supervision and extra-curricular activities. Using this approach the researcher is more able to maintain his or her detachment from subjects and take an outsider's view. He or she also sometimes finds it easier to see 'the familiar as strange' (Delamont, 1981) and explore aspects or patterns of social interaction which participants take for granted. Moreover, the researcher role enables him or her to observe in different settings within the school more easily. As a result the researcher is able to get a fuller, more rounded picture of the school or the part with which he or she is concerned. The danger, of course, is that the researcher fails to negotiate a non-threatening identity and is viewed with suspicion by subjects. As a result, subjects may change their behaviour to present themselves in particular ways to the researcher, and maybe even react to him or her with hostility. In order to avoid this researchers often place greater emphasis on the impression management strategies I discussed earlier.

CONCLUSION

These then are some of the issues which researchers must think about before they begin observational fieldwork in schools. To some extent at least they must clarify the focus of their investigations; they must decide which of the subjects, events, or behaviours they are interested in should actually be observed and recorded; and they must negotiate access to a position from which they can conduct their observations with the minimum of interference or disruption to the behaviour which routinely occurs in the setting. Of course, in many studies hard and fast decisions about these matters do not have to be made prior to the collection of any data. Indeed, it is often unwise to do this. In many research projects an element of flexibility is essential so that the researcher can respond to circumstances and events which occur during the fieldwork itself, and adjust his or her plans in the light of what is learned about the research setting.

NOTES

1. Where the aim of such research is explicitly evaluation the researcher may be expected to actually make such judgements.

2. On the principle and methods of random sampling see Bryman and Cramer, 1990, pp. 98–112.

3. Quota sampling is frequently used in market research and opinion polling where sampling frames of the relevant population are either unavailable or cumbersome to use.

4. The ethical issues surrounding these methods will be discussed in Chapter 6.

5. On the ethics of this issue see Denscombe and Aubrook (1992).

6. In research conducted in contexts other than schools the behaviour of subjects has sometimes been recorded with hidden cameras and/or microphones (see for example Haney, Banks and Zimbardo, 1973). Researchers have also sometimes made use of videotapes produced for non-research purposes (see for example Marsh, Rosser and Harre, 1978; Atkinson, 1984). I do not know of any examples of these methods being used in school research.

7. Hammersley and Atkinson (1995) argue that Willis (1977) erred in this way in his study of working class boys, but he did not join the group as a member.

3

Recording Observations

There are a number of ways in which observations can be recorded. The most comprehensive record is given by the use of video and/or audio equipment. This has become more feasible in recent years as technological advances have made equipment less obtrusive and more portable. Such advances have also considerably improved recording quality. More commonly, researchers, particularly those adopting qualitative approaches, record their observations in the form of field notes. Here researchers note down what they see and hear as fully as they can at the time or as soon as possible afterwards. Field notes typically contain a mixture of summary descriptions of events and verbatim records of conversations, and are stored in notebooks or files. Alternatively, where a more structured approach is adopted, researchers use standardized observation schedules which allow them to count, time or rate instances of pre-specified behaviour by entering codes or tallies.

Sometimes these methods are used in combination. Field notes, for example, are frequently supplemented by audio recording, the written notes focusing on description of physical movement and context whilst the audiotape provides the record of spoken language. Sometimes more structured observation schedules provide the space for more detailed qualitative description of behaviour in field note form. And often more structured observation schedules are used when the data on video- and audiotapes are analysed.

This chapter will examine the use of these different methods, and discuss their advantages and limitations.

VIDEO AND AUDIO RECORDING

The main advantage of using video and audio technology to record observations is that they provide a very detailed and accurate record. Obviously with audiotape this is restricted in the main to speech, whereas video also records physical movement and contextual information. This detail and accuracy is of great importance in studies concerned with the intricacies of language and social interaction, and video/audio recording has frequently been used in research focusing on these topics.

A second advantage is that it is possible to play back or, in the case of video, to freeze the record of behaviour, and this permits a more careful, flexible and complex analysis. The behaviour under consideration can be seen or heard repeatedly, scrutinized and discussed, and interpretations and coding during analysis can be checked. For this reason video and audio records can be especially useful in the pilot stages of observational studies where category systems and observation schedules are being designed.

A third advantage is that video or audio technology frees the researcher from at least some of the task of data recording. He or she can concentrate on recording observations of some particular aspect of the subject under consideration, for example contextual information, whilst the camera or tape recorder notes others. Alternatively he or she is more able to play a participant role in the situation if this is what is required, perhaps making notes retrospectively, but relying on the camera or tape recorder for the main record. Of course, this is why audio/video recording is so useful to teachers who are conducting research on their own practice. It is also possible, in principle, for the researcher to be absent from the scene altogether, thus eliminating that reactivity which derives directly from his or her physical presence (though, of course, subjects may still react to the presence of recording equipment, unless it is concealed).

Some of these advantages can be illustrated by considering a piece of research conducted by Swann and Graddol (1988) on gender inequalities in teacher–student classroom interaction. These researchers utilized videotapes of two sequences of classroom interaction in two primary schools. One sequence was a discussion between a teacher and a small group of 10–11-year-old students who were reporting the results of an experiment they had conducted. The other was a discussion between a teacher and eight 9–10-year-olds (four boys and four girls) following a television programme. Using the audio record Swann and Graddol transcribed the spoken language which occurred in the two discussions, and worked out how much each student talked. This was measured by counting for each student the number of words spoken, the number of speaking turns taken, and the number of interchanges with the teacher. They also counted the number of 'silent turns' by each student. These were 'occasion(s) on which no words were spoken but a response was clearly made, by means of conventional non-verbal sign such as a shrug of the shoulders or head nod' (p. 52). This information was obtained from the visual record provided by the videotape.

On the basis of these data Swann and Graddol concluded that boys tended to dominate teacher–student talk in the two sequences. However, the detailed audio/video record enabled them to take their research a stage further to investigate how this gender imbalance was produced. They focused their attention on the ways in which speaking turns were sequenced and synchronized by the teacher and students in the two discussions – what they term the 'turn exchange mechanism'. Drawing on the findings of discourse analysis, they argued that subtle cues are used by teachers and students to manage their verbal interaction. For example, teachers, who have the right to regulate classroom talk, frequently use their gaze to indicate which student

Teacher If you have a pendulum (.) which we established last week was a weight a mass (.) suspended from a string or whatever (.) and watch I'm holding it with my hand so it's at rest at the moment (.) what is it that makes the pendulum swing in a downward direction for instance till it gets to there? [1]? { (.) just watch it

Mathew { gravity

Teacher What is it Mathew? [2]

Mathew Gravity

Teacher { Yes (.) now we mentioned gravity when we were
Boy { ( ) }

Teacher actually doing the experiments but we didn't discuss it too much (.) OK so it's gravity then that pulls it down (.) what causes it to go up again at the other side? [3]

Boy { Force the force }
Boy { The string Miss } it gets up speed going down.

Teacher It gets up speed going { down (.) does } anyone know the word
Boy { (force) ( ) }

Teacher for it when you get up speed? [4] (.) as in a car when you press the pedal? [5]

Boy { accelerate }
Boy { momentum }

Teacher You get momentum (.) M { athew (.) } it accelerates going down
Mathew { ( ) }

Teacher doesn't it and it's the (.) energy the force that it builds up that takes it up the other side (.) watch (.) and see if it's the same (.) right· (.) OK (.) em (.) anything else you notice about that? [6]? (.) so it's gravity what about the moon? [7] (.) that's a bit tricky isn't it? [8] (.) is
  { there grav } ity on the moon? { [9]
Boys { (( ) }) { No it would float

Teacher There isn't gravity on the moon? [10] (.)

Several No

Mathew There is a certain amount

Teacher A certain amount Mathew? [11]

Mathew ( )
  { Seven } times less

Teacher You reckon it's seven? [12]

Boy Times less than on earth

Teacher Yes (.) well it's a it's a difficult figure to arrive at but it is between 6 and 7

Transcript Conventions:
↔↔↔ means gaze to boys { overlap (.) pause
──── means gaze to girls ( ) unclear

Figure 3.1 Transcript of teacher and pupil spoken language and gaze direction of teacher (from Swann and Graddol, 1988, pp. 53–4)

they wish to speak next. With this in mind, Swann and Graddol examined the discussions using the video record to note the direction of the teacher's gaze alongside the teacher's and students' spoken language. This is illustrated in the transcript shown in Figure 3.1.

In effect Swann and Graddol coded the teacher's gaze into three categories – directed at boys, directed at girls, and directed at neither – and calculated the proportion of 'pupil-directed gaze' directed to boys and girls. They found that 60 per cent was directed to boys and 40 per cent to girls in the first discussion, and in the second the proportions were 65 per cent and 35 per cent.[1] More significantly, they looked at the direction of the teacher's gaze at various points in teacher–student interchanges, and at how students obtained speaking turns by hand raising, calling out, and/or being selected by the teacher. In the first discussion they found that the teacher was more likely to be looking at boys at 'critical points, such as when a question is to be answered' (p. 56). In the second discussion they discovered that the teacher's gaze was more likely to be directed to boys at the beginning of interchanges, and that boys made bids to speak more frequently and earlier than girls. Moreover, the teacher was more likely to switch her gaze from girls to boys, than from boys to girls, at the beginning of an interchange. Swann and Graddol concluded that in both discussions the teacher's use of gaze favoured boys.

An example of a piece of research which relied on audio recording is a study by Tizard and Hughes (1984) which compared the learning experiences of young children at home and at nursery school. These researchers studied a sample of 30 three- and four-year-old girls from different social class backgrounds who were attending nursery schools in two LEAs. They recorded all the girls' conversations in three morning sessions at school and in two afternoons at home with their mothers, employing small radio microphones sewn into padded pockets on specially prepared dresses which the girls wore. Tizard and Hughes explain that the microphone was able to pick up everything the child said, and everything said to the child, within a range of about 15 feet, and that conversations could be transmitted to the tape recorder from up to 100 yards, thus allowing the child to play freely in the playground or garden and still be recorded. They say that, despite some technical problems, the quality of their recordings was good. In their pilot work the researchers tried to make recordings without an observer present, feeling that an observer unknown to the mother and child would be intrusive, especially in the home setting. However, they found that it was very difficult to make sense of their recordings, particularly in the nursery school, without the extra eyes and ears of an observer. Consequently an observer followed each child noting, as unobtrusively as possible, what she was doing, who she was speaking to and who spoke to her. These observations supplemented the detailed audio record which was later transcribed.

Tizard and Hughes' analysis of their transcriptions and observation notes revealed that in the home setting children often engaged in sophisticated language interactions with their mothers and were actively involved in complex learning experiences. In contrast, in the nursery school the children had far fewer and shorter conversations with adults, and these conversations were more often adult dominated, teachers speaking more than the children, taking more conversational turns and sustaining talk by means of questions. The researchers claim that sometimes teachers' questions appeared to facilitate children's cognitive development and language skills, but more often they seemed to induce confusion and reduce the amount of children's own questions and spontaneous talk to adults. Tizard and Hughes question the educational value of much of the teacher–child talk they recorded.

These two studies illustrate the advantages of employing video and audio methods to record observations. In both studies detailed and accurate records of speech, and, in the case of Swann and Graddol's study, of non-verbal communication were essential. The records enabled the researchers to scrutinize the interaction of the teachers and pupils they observed with great care, often going over sequences repeatedly to clarify their interpretations and take their analysis further. This detailed study revealed patterns of interaction which probably would not have been apparent to an ordinary observer, and the audio/visual record enhanced enormously the validity of the claims about these patterns which the researchers made.

But, of course, audio and video recording also has its drawbacks. First, the equipment, particularly video, is expensive and therefore adds considerably to the cost of the project. Second, permission to record in certain situations may be difficult to obtain, and a proposal involving such recording may make access more difficult to negotiate. This problem in part derives from feelings that the novelty of recording equipment will disrupt normal social interaction, but it also results from the sensitivity of some subjects about the potential use of observational data which is heightened by the accuracy of the audio/video record. Consequently observations may be limited to certain settings or sub-settings.

Where permission is obtained it is likely that reactivity will increase, particularly with video recording. Subjects are more likely to behave differently if they know their behaviour is being recorded on audio- or videotape, and where recording involves visible and obtrusive equipment, or the deliberate positioning of subjects, reactivity is likely to be more marked.

There are ways of minimizing this problem which are closely related to ideas we discussed in the previous chapter. One is to spend time allowing subjects to become accustomed to the presence of audio/video equipment so that it is less likely to be seen as unusual. Another is to decrease the obtrusiveness of the equipment by reducing its size. Most researchers select or modify equipment with this in mind, and they have been assisted in recent years by the miniaturization of audio/video recorders and microphones. Researchers also often position recording equipment out of the main line of view of subjects so they are less likely to be aware of its presence. In some cases they deliberately conceal recording equipment and record covertly which, of course, eliminates this form of reactivity altogether. They also, where possible, avoid moving subjects for the purpose of recording. However, all these techniques may have costs in terms of time or of the quality of the recordings which can be obtained.

Another problem with audio/video recording is that the researcher may be swamped with a large amount of data far beyond what is necessary or possible to analyse. When audio/video recording is possible there is a great temptation to avoid selection decisions and to try to record almost everything. The result is often a mass of data which is impossible to transcribe and analyse in the time available. The researcher therefore has to tailor carefully his or her sample of observations to fit the resources available for analysis. This usually means a relatively small sample which can be analysed in depth. Thus Swann and Graddol focused on only two sequences of classroom interaction, and Tizard and Hughes, in a larger scale project, restricted themselves to studying thirty children for just three sessions at school and two at home. They estimate that even this meant spending 4,000 hours collecting, transcribing and checking the data.

It is also important to realize that audio/video equipment cannot provide a complete record of behaviour. Its range, and capacity to record the details of complex interaction between a large number of subjects, is limited. For example, even behaviour that is 'in shot' may not be picked up by a video camera because it is obscured from view by furniture or other actors. Moreover, in comparison to the human observer, the flexibility of this equipment is poor. It is difficult to move the focus of microphone or camera quickly during recording. Nor can it provide information on the wider social context in which behaviour occurs. This must be provided by the more flexible eyes and ears of the researcher. We must also remember that, as with all technology, technical problems can occur – tapes run out, wires work loose, switches fail to work, and batteries run down (sometimes at the most inopportune moments). The result of these disasters is that important data can be lost.

Before we look at other methods there is one further issue related to the audio/video recording we must consider – whether, or when, these records should be transferred to paper and what form this should take. Sometimes it is useful to freeze the visual record provided by video and convert it into still photographs, drawings or diagramatic representations. Maps and diagrams, for example, can highlight key features of environmental context of behaviours under study, or summarize the distribution and movement of people in space. And still photographs or drawings can be useful in examining the detail of subjects' non-verbal communication. The latter technique was used in the study by Neill (1991) that I referred to in the previous chapter (see also Neill and Caswell, 1993).

But the most common type of transfer is the verbatim transcription of speech stored on audio- or videotape. Where the focus of the research requires detailed examination of the actual words spoken and of patterns in speech, a transcript of all, or at least relevant parts, of the audio/video record will probably be needed. A transcript has several advantages. First, it forces the researcher to listen closely to and think carefully about the data he or she has collected. In the process of transcribing the researcher becomes more familiar with the data, and often develops interesting and productive insights as a result. Transcription also eases analysis by cutting extraneous or irrelevant detail from the record. Moreover, it allows the researcher to locate and move between different parts of the record more easily, and enables him or her to annotate the data, noting down interpretations, questions, uncertainties, coding ideas, and so on. In fact, initial transcripts are often littered with the researcher's notes as he or she attempts to make sense of the data and begin the process of analysis. The transcript also enables the data to be broken down into segments which can be moved around, compared, categorized and coded in line with the researcher's developing analytical framework. Increasingly analysis of this sort of data employs computer software. At the moment this requires data in the written form, although in the future multimedia systems may permit the direct use of audio/video records in this way. A final advantage is that transcription allows some of the data, or the whole data base, if it is small enough, to be presented in the final written report of the research. This data can be presented as illustration or as evidential support for the claims made in the report, and permits readers to assess the validity of the claims which are made in the research.

At the same time, transcription is enormously time consuming and frequently frustrating. Tizard and Hughes (1984), for example, explain that one hour of their school tapes took nine hours to transcribe and an extra three hours to check and add notes about context. In some studies it is unnecessary to transcribe all data which has been collected on audio/videotape. It may be possible to proceed with analysis on the basis of relatively short written summaries of verbal behaviour, together with transcription of relevant sections which require more careful scrutiny. And where the focus of the investigation requires the counting or timing of particular behaviours, systematic analysis can be conducted directly from the audio/video record onto some sort of observation schedule.

The other point to bear in mind is that transcription involves selection and therefore a loss of data. Obviously the transcripts of speech from video do not include the visual record (though summaries can be produced to go alongside the talk), but transcripts also often reduce the complexity of speech by simplifying or ignoring aspects of pronunciation and intonation. These aspects of the data can sometimes be extremely important in understanding meaning, and their removal may be a source of error. Transcription also involves interpretation and sometimes the transcriber may read meanings into speech, especially where it is difficult to decipher, which were not those communicated by the speakers, thus again introducing error. This is a strong argument against using secretaries or assistants, who are unfamiliar with the situation under study, to transcribe tapes. Such individuals may also lack the researcher's strong commitment to the accuracy of the record and therefore be more likely to make mistakes. But, of course, assistants may ease the researcher's work burden considerably, and, if available, might be used to produce a first draft of a transcript which can then be corrected and filled out by the researcher.

If transcripts are to be produced what form should they take? This again depends on the focus of the investigation. As I have said, any transcription involves loss of information and the researcher has to decide what particular features of the speech it is necessary to include given the research focus.[2] If, for example, he or she is interested in the meanings communicated only by the actual words spoken a relatively simple transcript which reproduces what was said and who said it (or the social category of the speaker) may be sufficient. An example is shown in Figure 3.2 which is taken from the research conducted by Wragg (1993) that I mentioned in Chapter 1. In this part of the study the researchers were interested in the techniques used by teachers to explain concepts to children. Here one teacher is discussing what an insect is.

Teacher	Is a bird an insect?
Pupil 1	No, that's silly.
Teacher	Why?
Pupil 1	Well, it's too small. A bird's bigger.
Teacher	So all insects are small, then, and all birds are big?
Pupil 2	No, you can have little birds . . . and big insects.
Pupil 3	It's got the wrong number of legs.
Teacher	Why, how many does an insect have?
Pupil 3	Six.
Pupil 1	No it doesn't. It's eight. A spider's got eight legs.
Pupil 3	A spider's not an insect.
Teacher	Well, let's clear that one up first.

Figure 3.2   Simple transcript from Wragg, 1993, pp. 125–6

Transcripts like this often 'tidy up' speech leaving out things like pauses, hesitations, overlaps between speakers, intonation, accent or dialect. But sometimes these sorts of detail are important to the focus of the research, and attempts are made to represent them in various ways. An example is contained in Figure 3.3 which shows one way of doing this. It is an extract from the transcript produced by French and French (1984) in their study of gender inequality in classroom talk. I have also included the researchers' key of transcript conventions. Other transcription systems include information about accent or dialect by representing speech more phonetically (see, for example, Hewitt, 1986), and about intonation by using symbols which represent pitch and loudness levels and movements (see, for example, Brazil, Coultard and Johns, 1980).

FIELD NOTES

Where audio/video recording is not possible, researchers interested in the qualitative features of the behaviour which occurs in schools generally record their observations in the form of field notes. Field notes usually provide a fairly

Transcript Conventions

1. Participants' identities appear on the left, as in a play script. The teacher is identified as T. Pupils' names appear where they are known. Where a pupil's identity is not known he/she appears as P1, P2 etc. Where pupils speak collectively they are identified as Ps.

2. Participants' speech appears to the right of their identities, again as in a play script.

3. Speech enclosed in single parentheses indicates that the transcriber thinks that this is what was said but is not 100 per cent sure, e.g. (what do you get up at that time for)?

4. Asterisks enclosed in parentheses indicate that a speaker said something but that the transcriber was unable to decipher it properly. The asterisks represent the number of syllables heard, e.g. (* * *).

5. Empty parentheses indicate that a speaker said something but that the transcriber was unable to hear even how many syllables were uttered.

6. Speech enclosed in double parentheses represents a description of some relevant activity, e.g. ((shrugs)), ((various pupils call out)).

7. A colon following a syllable indicates that the syllable was pronounced in a long, drawn-out style, e.g. no:

8. Pauses between utterances are timed in seconds and tenths of seconds, e.g. (1.5) represents a pause of one and half seconds. A full stop between parentheses indicates an immeasurably brief pause.

9. An equals sign may be used to indicate 'latched' speech, i.e. where a second speaker comes in immediately the first speaker has stopped speaking, e.g.
   T.   what animals have you got?
   Tom   erm=
   T.   = you've got your parakeet
   Equals signs may also be used to indicate that a speaker is continuing with his/her turn when it has perhaps been interrupted by a second speaker, e.g.
   T.   do you do that before you come to school ⌈everyday=
   Matthew   ⌊yeah
   T.   =do you? (.) oh well then . . .

10. Dashes may be used to indicate that a speaker hesitates or stammers over a word, e.g.
   T.   in the evenings – there's three evenings a week for example when I – when I . . .

11. Where participants' speech overlaps, a square bracket indicates the onset of overlap, e.g.
   Andrew   it would be exactly⌈the same
   Γ.   ⌊perhaps then

Transcript

Extract 10

1.	T.	right put your hands down ⌈(0.4) if I (* * *)=
2.	Tom	⌊I'd rather (* * *)
3.	T.	=Marie and Nina?
4.	Marie	only sometimes
5.	T.	not on Mondays though (.) we're talking about Mondays
6.		in particular aren't we?
7.		(1.0)
8.	Andrew	Sir I like coming to school on Tuesdays Wednesdays
9.		and Fridays
10.	Wayne	Tuesday's swimming
11.	P1	Sir I like– ((at this point several pupuls begin to call out and it is impossible to distinguish individuals))
12.	T.	alright now look if you want anything (.) sh sh if you
13.		want to say anything now you've got to put your hand up
14.		otherwise we'll have twenty nine people trying to talk
15.		all at once and (that'll never do)

Figure 3.3 More complex transcript from French and French, 1984, pp. 132 and 134

detailed record of the researcher's observations of behaviour and the physical and social context in which it occurs; and, as the concern is often to explore the perspectives and interpretations of social actors, they also often include records of the researcher's conversations, discussions and interviews.

One of the problems researchers face here is deciding what to record. It is very difficult to observe and record simultaneously, and impossible to record all the sensory information coming in. Selection is inevitable. What the researcher decides to observe and record depends in the main on the focus of the research and the stage the research has reached. The particular questions the researcher chooses to address will encourage him or her to ignore some information and note down only what he or she sees as relevant or potentially relevant. However, in the early stages of a research project the focus may be unclear and there may be considerable shifts in it as the research progresses. As a result researchers often adopt a relatively open-ended approach at first, making a broad and general record of what is happening, whilst making more detailed records of incidents which seem particularly interesting or revealing. As the research progresses, and the focus becomes clearer and narrower, researchers make more detailed records of the particular events or behaviours they are interested in.

As Hammersley and Atkinson (1995) note, there is an inevitable trade off in these decisions between depth and breadth. The more detailed the record that is made of particular behaviours the narrower is the range of behaviours which can be recorded. What is important is that decisions *are* made so that the recording of observations is manageable. There is a danger, particularly where the researcher's focus is unclear, in trying to record too much. The result is usually frustration at a perceived inability to keep up the record, and inconsistency in the record itself as the focus flits from one bright idea to another.

Another way in which this problem can be resolved is by sampling. As I pointed out in the last chapter, researchers often concentrate their observations on a sample of people, places, events or times. For example, the researcher may select a sample of lessons to observe, and focus his or her observations during these lessons on a sample of children, recording the nature of their behaviour at sampled times. This sampling may be guided by theoretical concerns or a desire to get a representative picture.

Another question which must be addressed is *when* field notes are made. It is preferable for field notes to be made as soon as possible after observation. The longer this is left the more is forgotten and the greater is the chance of inaccuracies and biases creeping in. Sometimes it is possible to take notes as observations are made. This is often the case with classroom research. In my experience teachers, if they are willing to allow a researcher to observe their lessons, usually do not mind him or her taking notes. Taking notes in the classroom generally seems to be seen as a legitimate activity, perhaps because teachers in this context feel more publicly accountable or because people like inspectors and tutors of student teachers frequently engage in the same activity. What we have to remember though is that note taking may affect the teachers', and perhaps the students', perceptions of the researcher. They will probably be seen as more threatening, and this may affect the way teachers and students behave.

However, note taking at the time of observation will be difficult, if not impossible, if the researcher is playing a participant role. Here the researcher's immediate attention and energy must be put into playing the participant role itself, and this usually leaves little time for recording observations. The exception is when writing is a normal part of the participant role, as it might be, for example, in a meeting or an in-service training session. In these circumstances it is possible for the researcher to make notes under the cloak of the participant role.

There are also situations in schools where social norms do not permit note taking. For example, it would probably be considered unacceptable to take notes in the staff room. One solution here is to take notes secretly. Hammersley (1980), for example, jotted down brief notes on his newspaper when observing in the staff room of the school he studied. And in my research (Foster, 1990a) I was lucky that a staff work area adjoined the staff room. From here I could sit and listen to staff room conversations and record anything which I felt was important whilst giving the impression that I was working.

But usually where note taking at the time is not possible researchers must record their observations in another context some time after they are made. Often they are written in the evenings or in periods of free time when observation is not important. It is essential that time is made to do this otherwise significant information can be forgotten or distorted. Indeed, it is important that researchers take breaks from observation, not just to catch up on note taking, but to organize, examine and analyse data and reflect on the research itself. These breaks are essential to plan future data collection effectively and also to recuperate from the stresses and strains of fieldwork. There is a danger that researchers spend too much time in schools observing and too little time recording and analysing their data. As Lacey (1976) pointed out, there is a tendency to fall into the 'it's happening elsewhere or when I'm not there syndrome'. Researchers sometimes feel that they have to be in schools all the time and preferably in several places in the school at once. If they succumb to this temptation the result is observations which are forgotten, and therefore wasted, and/or an overwhelming mass of unanalysed data.

Field notes vary considerably in form, and individual researchers usually develop their own particular style and organization. Some researchers record their observations in longhand, others write them in their own idiosyncratic shorthand and type them up in detail later. Some make extensive use of diagrams, especially to record the organization of physical space, others prefer the narrative form. Some researchers make their notes in note books, others use files from which pages can easily be taken for copying or reorganization. Some restrict their field notes to accounts of what they have seen and heard, others include, usually in separate sections, speculations about the meaning of behaviour and the intentions of the actors, and their own analytic or methodological reflections.

Whatever the style or format, it is essential that notes contain basic contextual information – date, time, place, etc. – and any other information about the context of an event or behaviour which may be relevant. It is also important to distinguish clearly between verbatim records of speech, summaries of events, and interpretations, and to note any uncertainties in the account. Most researchers also give some space in field notes to an assessment of reactivity and to methodological reflection in general.

Once notes have been made they must be organized in such a way that information can be located and retrieved fairly easily. This requires some sort of cataloguing and indexing system, perhaps using a computer system. The organization of data into sections, themes and categories for this purpose is part of the analysis of the data which proceeds alongside data collection. I will discuss this process more fully in the next chapter.

What, then, are the main advantages of field notes as a method of recording observations? Their main advantage over more structured methods (which we will discuss in a moment) is flexibility. Researchers are not restricted to a pre-defined focus or tied to allocating behaviours to pre-defined categories. Their focus can vary in response to unanticipated events which occur in the field, and to the analysis of the data and the development of theoretical ideas. Observations can also be noted in differing ways, varying in detail and emphasis according to the stage and focus of the research.

A second advantage is that field notes provide a much fuller, more rounded record of events than the numbers provided by more structured methods. The narrative account recorded in field notes gives much more detail of the qualitative nature and sequences of behaviour, and of the physical, social and cultural context in which they occur. Moreover, the attention to the interpretations and perspectives of social actors allows a fuller appreciation of meanings in play in particular situations. These, combined with the story genre used in these accounts, give readers a much greater feel for what actually happens in a situation and why.

When compared to audio/video recording the great advantage is that making field notes is less obtrusive, and reactivity may therefore be less of a problem. The only equipment necessary is paper and pencil, and in many situations in schools sitting jotting down notes is a fairly unremarkable activity, and is unlikely in itself to disrupt routine behaviour very much. Of course, in some circumstances field notes do not have to be made at the time of observation, and the researcher is therefore freed to play a more participant role. They can also be made secretly in situations where the open recording of observations would be highly disruptive or where permission would not be given.

Again let me illustrate some of these points by considering a couple of examples of research in which observations have been recorded using field notes. The first is a study of the work of headteachers conducted by Hall,

Mackay and Morgan (1986). The researchers observed 15 secondary school headteachers for a day, and then conducted a more in-depth study of 4 heads, observing them for an average of 174 hours each over the course of a year. The researchers followed the heads in their normal daily work recording their observations in abbreviated, longhand notes. Whilst observing, they tried to be as unobtrusive as possible, remaining in the background and avoiding social interaction. Figure 3.4 shows an example of the sort of data they collected. The data were used to explore the overall features of headteachers' work and details of the tasks they performed and how they performed them.

Field notes provided these researchers with a detailed running record of the behaviour of the headteachers and of the contexts in which they operated. Given the exploratory nature of the study and the concern to examine the idiosyncratic nature of each head's role performance, more structured recording methods would have been inappropriate (although some quantitative findings did emerge from the analysis, such as the amount of time headteachers spent on different tasks). Video, and to some extent audio, recording would have been very obtrusive and probably impractical given the movement of the heads around the schools. Moreover, they would have given the researchers large amounts of material to transcribe which would have increased considerably the time required for the project. Such data was probably unnecessary anyway given the relatively general focus of the study.

Another example of observational research employing field notes is the study by Burgess (1983) of a Catholic comprehensive school I mentioned in Chapter 1 (see Burgess, 1984 for more detail on the methodology of the study). Burgess was much more a participant observer than the researchers we have just considered. He spent 16 months in the school and taught part time as well as conducting the research. Each day he recorded his observations of the events, in and out of the classroom, which he observed and/or participated in, and noted his conversations with teachers and students. Sometimes he made these notes as he observed, but more often they were written in brief interludes during the day or in the evenings.

Adopting an interactionist approach, Burgess focused on the way in which different conceptions of school values and norms were negotiated by teachers and students, and went on to look in detail at teaching in the 'Newsom Department', a department for 'less-able pupils' where he taught most of his lessons. In his book reporting the research Burgess frequently quotes from his field notes. Figure 3.5 shows an example. Here he describes a meeting of the Newsom teachers which took place at the beginning of the academic year when it was discovered that little of the equipment ordered at the end of the previous year had arrived, that rooms which the teachers planned to use for practical work were unavailable and that additional groups had been allocated to the teachers.

Burgess uses stories like this to illustrate the teachers' approach to their work in the Newsom Department. He argues that the teachers developed a very different way of working with Newsom students from that in other areas

9.00

The phone went, a mother wanting to know if she could take her eleven-year-old daughter into the school, as they had just moved into the district. He advised her that they were full in the first year and she would have to make a separate appeal to the county.

> You have an eleven-year-old child and you want to change? You have to write to the chief education officer. The decision on first year entries are made at county hall not at individual schools. Do you live in my area? (No.) I should say that the chances aren't strong. The number you want to ring is . . . schools department, then ask for a personal call to Mr Pearson and he'll tell you exactly what to do. Why have you left it so late? . . . Because all these things are sorted out much earlier. If the Authority says yes that's fine by me. If they say no I have to abide by that. . . . Goodbye.

He jotted down different requests staff made earlier in the entrance hall; to go on a course in school time; to look at a new homework book for history. He went out into the corridor to chivvy some girls who were dawdling their way to the assembly hall.

> Come on girls, hurry up (louder). Come on, you're holding everyone up. Take your coat off. (Pulling a boy's tie out of his shirt.) That's better.

9.05

When there were no more pupils in the corridor, he returned to his room to give the daily messages out over the tannoy. They were relayed to all assembly points in the upper and lower school building. He praised the tidiness of the school, 'please keep it like that'; gave details of CSE oral exams, room changes, rehearsals for Showboat, netball practices; read out the results of matches and details of the Drama Club and Seekers' Club meetings; 'finally, don't forget point number one I started with. The place is looking much nicer. Keep it that way.'

9.10

Notices finished, he crossed between the buildings, telling off some latecomers on the way, and waited at the back of the lower school hall, where the head of lower school was addressing the pupils. Taking his place at the front, Mr Shaw congratulated the twenty-five pupils in turn who came up to receive their commendations for work and behaviour during the year. When he finished, he asked the children,

> Now, I don't think I'll have to ask this question more than once again. How many here have now got at least one commendation? (Nearly every hand in the hall went up, the whole of the first year.) 'That's marvellous. Let's hope it's everyone.'

9.35

On his way back to his office, Maureen Osmond (head of geography) caught up with him to tell him about her unsuccessful job interview the previous Friday. He commiserated, and told her, although she had not got the job, he had heard that her interview went very well.

9.40

Outside his room a dozen or so children were queuing to collect distinction certificates. He took a pile from his desk and asked each pupil in, shaking hands and congratulating them.

9.50

Vivien Collins (commerce) came in, worried about the insurance forms that all employers were now expected to fill in for work experience pupils. Mr Shaw sat down with her at the coffee table and they discussed the difficulties. He suggested local businesses who might be interested in taking on some of the pupils, which she noted down.

Figure 3.4 Field notes from Hall, Mackay and Morgan, 1986, pp. 21–2

The group met in Sylvia's room which had been used to store materials for the Newsom department. It contained piles of departmental stock and equipment. One book case was crammed with pink exercise books which had been ordered for Newsom work in the previous year and never used. In the far corner was a pile of games and boxes of unopened Childwall project material which appeared never to have been moved since they were originally dumped in that position.

Although Sylvia was no longer in charge of the department she still assumed control. She placed chairs around in front of her desk, behind which she sat to address Tony, Keith, Terry and myself. Sylvia posed the problems and waited for our answers. 'How are we going to get rooms? How are we going to obtain equipment? What are we going to do with the pupils in extra lessons?' she asked. Terry was the first to respond. She considered that we might subdivide the pupils again and allocate further practical work. Sylvia agreed. She said she could keep one group fully occupied tidying up her study for part of the term, after which she suggested Tony and Keith could come along with a group of boys to decorate it. The idea sparked off debate. It was evident from the expression on Tony's face that he was not prepared to support this idea. He remarked, 'I think there is already too much practical work in the course.' Terry disagreed claiming that practical activities were the only way in which pupils could be involved in the work. However, Tony managed to persuade the others that more 'theory' work should be done and volunteered to take this on himself. It was reluctantly agreed that this was the only way to solve the problem of inadequate rooms and a lack of equipment.

Keith Dryden had said little up to this point. It was evident that he was quietly fuming. He was still not satisfied with the 'solution' as it was impossible for him to work without adequate rooms and equipment. This started Terry off again because she did not have the equipment which had been ordered for her screen printing. By this time some three-quarters of an hour had passed and Sylvia attempted to sum up our decisions. She said he would be contacting the deputy head to get further rooms for our groups. However, Keith doubted if this would result in any satisfaction. The bell went to signal the end of the 'lesson' and we heard a door burst open followed by shouting and cheering as our Newsom pupils ran out of the block towards the school gate. It was the end of the afternoon. We finished our meeting and left Sylvia in her room. Keith walked away grumbling about the lack of provision. 'How can we teach properly if things are like this?' he asked. We all agreed that something had to be done. Keith remarked, 'Sylvia's all right but we shouldn't leave everything for her to do, otherwise it'll be a mess.' He and Tony therefore agreed to contact the deputy head separately to get further rooms so that we could begin teaching in the second week of term.

Figure 3.5   Field notes from Burgess, 1983, pp. 193–4

of the school. Their academic and behavioural expectations were much lower, and they taught a supposedly more relevant curriculum based around liberal ideas and practical skills, in which considerable control was given to students.

From the standpoint of his participant role, Burgess gives vivid and detailed accounts of events within the school and department. He also recounts his own socialization into the culture of Newsom teaching. His descriptions often take the form of narrative 'social dramas' which bring the day-to-day reality of the school alive for the reader. Field notes provided a flexible means by which Burgess could record his perceptions of the events he observed and experienced. Given his aim and focus, structured methods were inappropriate, and video/audio recording would probably have worked against the development of his participant identity which was such a significant source of relevant data.

These studies highlight the advantages of recording observations in field notes. There are, however, a number of problems with this technique that must be recognized. The first relates to the inevitable selectivity involved in observation and recording. The ambiguity of focus (especially in the early stages) of this type of research may mean that researchers may fail to record relevant data. Alternatively, they may record data inconsistently, so that relevant data is collected in some contexts but not in others. This may result in data which is unrepresentative of the particular population with which the researcher is concerned. More seriously, perhaps, there is a danger that the researcher consciously or unconsciously selects observations which support preconceived ideas or initial impressions, and ignores those which do not. Alternatively, he or she may be drawn to the exotic or unusual and neglect the routine or mundane (see Sadler, 1982). Such subjectivity, which is made more likely by the unsystematic nature of selection in much research of this type, can be a serious source of error (see Chapter 5).

It is also important to emphasize that our human tendency to seek and impose meaning on the world means that what is observed is interpreted. Interpretations are made on the basis of the researcher's existing knowledge, conceptual framework and cultural standpoint. This is often evident in researcher's field notes, especially where they contain summary descriptions of events.The notes made by Burgess shown in Figure 3.5, for example, reveal this sort of interpretive work. He sees the events described in the early part of the account as precipitating a 'minor crisis' for the Newsom teachers, putting the students together to see a film 'which had been found in the stock cupboard that morning' is seen as 'entertaining' (presumably rather than educating) them, the coming together of teachers is perceived as a 'meeting' in which Sylvia 'assumed control', and so on. Here we can see how Burgess made sense of the behaviour he observed, and allocated it to summary descriptive categories in his account.

In many accounts we can be reasonably confident that the researcher's interpretation of events is accurate in the sense of being congruent with those of the participants. But in some circumstances this may not be the case. For various reasons the researcher may misinterpret what occurs, particularly where the behaviour is complex or when he or she is unfamiliar with the social situation and the meanings which are in play. The resulting account will therefore distort the 'real' nature of events. This point was brought graphically home to me in my own research (Foster, 1990a) in a multi-ethnic school. I observed a situation in which a white adolescent boy called an Afro-Caribbean boy a 'nigger'. I initially interpreted this as an instance of racial abuse and recorded it as such in my field notes. However, I discovered later that the two boys were the best of friends and regularly swapped racial insults as a form of camaraderie. My initial observation was clearly a misinterpretation of the real meaning of this behaviour from the boys' point of view. This is, of course, one reason why researchers often check their interpretation of events with those of participants.

Another point to note here is that the researcher's use of descriptive categories in field notes is sometimes not made explicit. Often categories are not defined and procedures for allocating instances of behaviour to categories are not specified, as happens with more structured approaches. It is possible, therefore, that categories are used inconsistently, making data unreliable. These features of ethnographic observation and recording, combined with the idiosyncratic ways in which such research is sometimes conducted, mean that it is very difficult to compare data collected by different researchers in different contexts.

Finally, we must also note the problems which can occur when there is a time lapse between observation and the making of the written record. The longer this is the more detail will be lost from the researcher's memory and the greater are the chances of distortion occurring from other sources.

MORE STRUCTURED RECORDING

In examining the research by Swann and Graddol (1988) earlier in the chapter we saw how video records could be used to produce quantitative data. But sometimes the aims of a research project, and the practical and resource constraints impinging on it, require that such data is produced from observations recorded 'live'. In these sorts of project the aim is to produce numerical data on the incidence, duration or maybe quality of particular behaviours or events from recordings made at the time in the form of tallies or codings. As I explained in Chapter 1, this is often the case in large scale projects, employing a number of researchers, where the aim is to make comparisons between teachers, departments, schools, etc. and to seek for widespread patterns in educational phenomena. But it is also the case in smaller scale case studies where quantitative data are needed on particular aspects of school life.

In this type of research clear decisions must be made before data collection begins so that standardized and consistent procedures can be adopted.[3] These are discussed in detail by Croll (1986) and I will draw heavily on his discussion here. First, the researcher must specify the behavioural focus of the research. He or she must define clearly the type of behaviour to be recorded and how instances of this behaviour can be distinguished from other behaviour. Second, the researcher must decide how instances of this behaviour are to be categorized. This involves defining the key characteristics of categories and specifying the procedures by which instances of behaviour can be allocated to categories.

These decisions can be illustrated by looking at part of the observation recording system developed for the Primary Science Teaching Action Research (STAR) project (Cavendish et al., 1990). These researchers focused on the nature of the activity of sampled pupils during the teaching of primary science. They divided pupil activity into three main categories – non-talk activity, involvement in talk indicating key science process skills, and involvement in other talk. These categories were then sub-divided into the categories shown in Figure 3.6.

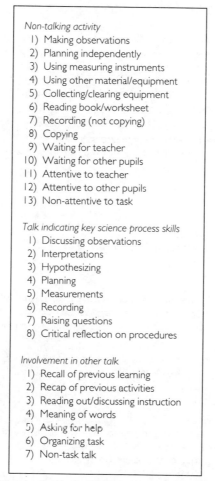

Non-talking activity
1) Making observations
2) Planning independently
3) Using measuring instruments
4) Using other material/equipment
5) Collecting/clearing equipment
6) Reading book/worksheet
7) Recording (not copying)
8) Copying
9) Waiting for teacher
10) Waiting for other pupils
11) Attentive to teacher
12) Attentive to other pupils
13) Non-attentive to task

Talk indicating key science process skills
1) Discussing observations
2) Interpretations
3) Hypothesizing
4) Planning
5) Measurements
6) Recording
7) Raising questions
8) Critical reflection on procedures

Involvement in other talk
1) Recall of previous learning
2) Recap of previous activities
3) Reading out/discussing instruction
4) Meaning of words
5) Asking for help
6) Organizing task
7) Non-task talk

Figure 3.6 Pupil activity categories used in the STAR project (Cavendish *et al.*, 1990)

Here then we have the behavioural focus of pupil activity in science lessons broken down initially into 3 categories and then into 28 categories. It is possible then to regard the concept of pupil activity as either a 3 category variable or a 28 category variable. Alternatively, we can see the three main categories as variables in themselves with 13, 8 and 7 categories respectively. All pupil talk was also categorized into two dichotomous variables – whether the pupil was actively or not actively involved, and whether or not the teacher was involved in the dialogue. The researchers developed definitions for these categories and coding rules to enable instances of pupil activity to be coded under the appropriate categories. These were set out in a manual which provided detailed guidance for observers. An extract from this is shown in Figure 3.7

Sometimes category systems involve rating. An example is contained in

1 *Discussing observations*
   Refers to description of characteristics of objects or situations which children have directly
   perceived through their senses. May involve comparison between objects and events, such as
   similarities and differences. Includes descriptions of the order in which events took place. Includes
   descriptions of observations in which a pattern exists ('the biggest went the furthest, then the
   next biggest and the smallest went the smallest distance') as opposed to a description of the
   pattern ('the bigger they are the further they go').

   Examples
   P.   When you push the blocks down they all float back up.
   T.   Does everyone agree with that . . . when you push them down they all float back up?
   P.   Yes.

   T.   Now, what have you found out that's the same about your blocks?
   P.1   . . . they all float level.
   P.2   . . . they don't dip over . . . like that (gestures with hands).
   T.   That's a lovely observation, anything else . . . ?

   T.   Look very closely at the way the blocks float and their weights . . . can you see any pattern
         there?
   P.   They're all in the same order.
   T.   Can you say anything else . . . can you put that another way?
   T.   What can you tell me about the weight of the block and the way it floated?
   P.   The lightest block floated best . . . and the heaviest block was the worst floater.
   T.   Does everyone agree . . . do you think it has something to do with weight?

2 *Interpretation*
   Drawing a conclusion or inference for which there is some (though not necessarily sufficient)
   evidence in the children's findings. Identifying a pattern linking observations or data. Interpolating
   or extrapolating from observed data whether or not the pattern which justifies it is stated.

   Examples
   T.   Here's a graph showing how fast the soluble aspirin dissolved at different temperatures.
         Tell me, then, what is the connection between temperature of the water and the time for
         the aspirin to dissolve?
   P.   As the water gets hotter, the aspirin dissolves quicker.

Figure 3.7   Examples of category definitions and coding rules used in the STAR project (Cavendish *et al.*,
1990, p. 106)

research by Pascal, Bertram and Ramsden (1994) on the quality of children's
experiences in various preschool settings. These researchers argue that a child's
'involvement' in preschool activities is a significant indicator of the quality of
his or her learning experiences and therefore used a measure called the Leuven
Involvement Scale for Young Children, developed by Laevers (1994a and b).
Researchers using this measure observed individual sampled children for 2
minute periods focusing on the presence or absence of 'involvement signals' –
concentration, energy, creativity, facial expression and posture, persistence,
precision, reaction time and language. (For details on the nature of these
signals, see Pascal, 1994.) On this basis they rated the children's involvement
on the five point scale shown in Figure 3.8. This system clearly requires a

Level 1. No Activity
Activity at this level can be simple stereotypic repetitive and passive. The child is absent and displays no energy. There is an absence of cognitive demand. The child characteristically may stare into space. N.B. This may be a sign of inner concentration.

Level 2. A Frequently Interrupted Activity
The child is engaged in an activity but half of the observed period includes moments of non-activity in which the child is not concentrating and is staring into space. There may be interruptions frequently in the child's concentration, but his/her involvement is not enough to return to the activity.

Level 3. Mainly Continuous Activity
The child is busy at an activity but it is at a routine level and the real signals for involvement are missing. There is some progress but energy is lacking and concentration is at a routine level. The child can be easily distracted.

Level 4. Continuous Activity with Intense Moments
The child's activity has intense moments during which activities at Level 3 can come to have special meaning. Level 4 is reserved for the kind of activity seen in those intense moments, and can be deduced from the 'Involvement signals'. This level of activity is resumed after interruptions. Stimuli, from the surrounding environment, however attractive, cannot seduce the child away from the activity.

Level 5. Sustained Intense Activity
The child shows continuous and intense activity revealing the greatest *involvement*. In the observed period not all the signals for involvement need be there, but the essential ones must be present: concentration, creativity, energy and persistence. This intensity must be present for almost all the observation period.

Figure 3.8 Leuven Involvement Scales for Young Children (LIS-YC) (from Pascal, Bertram and Ramsden, 1994)

relatively high degree of judgement by the observer, in recognizing 'involvement signals' and in rating involvement, which increases the potential for inconsistency, especially when large numbers of observers are used. However, Pascal, Bertram and Ramsden (1994) argue that the reliability of the scale has proved to be quite high. (A similar system of rating is used in school inspections except here whole lessons are rated in terms of the quality of teaching and learning.)

Another decision which must also be made with most systematic observation systems is whether the researcher wants to record the frequency and/or duration of particular behaviours. How often a person does something may clearly be different from how long they spend doing it. Decisions also have to be made about whether to record when a behaviour occurs in time and where it occurs in a particular sequence of behaviours. There are three main possibilities here.

First is some sort of continuous recording. Here a time chart is used and the type of behaviour which is observed is coded continuously on the chart. When the behaviour changes a new code is used from the time of the change. This type of recording allows the observer to locate behaviours in time and in sequences, and to record their frequency and duration. We have already seen a simple example of this type of coding in the research by Swann and Graddol (1988) (see Figure 3.1), although this was not done live. Swann and Graddol coded the teacher's gaze into three categories – directed at boys, directed at girls and directed at neither – and indicated their coding using differently marked lines above their transcript of teacher and pupil talk.

One of the few substantial examples of the use of continuous recording is research on primary school teachers' working day conducted in the late 1960s (Hilsum and Cane, 1971). These researchers observed 129 teachers for one or two days each and focused on the amount of time teachers spent on different activities. Teachers' activities were coded into 55 categories, ranging from 'teaching' to 'marking' (without interaction with the pupil) to 'playground duty'. The researchers, using stop watches, recorded the appropriate category on a time chart with rows representing minutes divided into 5 second intervals, changing the category when the teacher's activity changed and indicating continuity with a single line.

Unfortunately continuous recording is limited in several respects. It can be difficult to use where the type of behaviour of interest changes frequently and rapidly, as is often the case in classroom interaction. In these circumstances live continuous recording is impractical unless very broad categories are employed. It is also difficult to record more than one variable or category of a variable at a time, unless more than one observer is used. Moreover, if the nature of the behaviour being observed is ambiguous and coding decisions cannot be made until some time after the behaviour has begun, continuous recording is usually impossible. For these reasons the researchers in the STAR project decided not to use this system even though it would have provided them with a more accurate record than they subsequently obtained of the incidence, duration, time location and sequencing of the different activities.

A second possibility is time (or point) sampling. As I explained in the previous chapter, this usually involves coding the behaviour which is occurring at regular points in time – say every 30 seconds or every minute. Assuming that, taken together, these points are representative of others, we can estimate the proportion of time taken up by particular behaviours. Using this method it is also possible to establish when during the observation period particular behaviours occur. Perhaps more significantly, the gap between observation and recording allows the observer to code a relatively large number of variables. However, it is not possible to discover the frequency of behaviours (except a minimum frequency) since the sample is of times rather than events; nor does it permit the recording of the sequences of events within which behaviour occurs. It is also important to note that this system tends to conflate frequency and duration – a large number of short instances of particular behaviours can produce the same record as a smaller number of long ones.

Despite these problems time sampling is commonly used in educational research. One example is the ORACLE project (Galton, Simon and Croll,

COOP TK	Fully involved and co-operating on approved task work (e.g. reading)
COOP R	Fully involved and co-operating on approved routine work (e.g. sharpening a pencil)
DSTR	Non-involved and totally distracted from all work
DSTR OBSR	Non-involved and totally distracted from all work by the observer
DSRP	Non-involved and aggressively disrupting work of other pupil(s)
HPLY	Non-involved and engaging in horseplay with other pupil(s)
WAIT TCHR	Waiting to interact with the teacher
CODS	Partially co-operating and partially distracted from approved work
INT TCI IR	Interested in teacher's activity or private interaction with other pupil(s)
INT PUP	Interested in the work of other pupil(s)
WOA	Working on an alternative activity which is not approved work
RIS	Not coded because the target is responding to internal stimuli
NOT OBS	Not coded because the target is not observed for some reason
NOT LIST	Not coded because the target's activity is not listed

Figure 3.9   Pupil activity codes used in the ORACLE project (Galton, Simon and Croll, 1980, p. 13)

1980) I have referred to in earlier chapters. In the part of this research which focused on pupils, observers coded the behaviour of sampled pupils at 25 second intervals. The pupil's activity was coded by ticking one of the 14 categories shown in Figure 3.9.

The observers also recorded information on a number of other category variables at the same point in time – the pupil's location, the teacher's activity and location, the pupil's interaction with other pupils (including the pupil's role in this interaction, the mode of interaction, the task of the other pupils, the sex and number of other pupils), and the pupil's interaction with adults (including again the pupil's role in this interaction, which adult the interaction was with, what the interaction was about, and the setting in which the interaction occurred (see Boydell and Jasman, 1983 for details). Using this record the researchers were able to say, for example, what proportion of class time pupils spent on particular activities, in particular locations, in particular types of interaction with teachers and other pupils, and so on. And, as we can see, the researchers were able to record information on a large number of variables which could be cross-referenced and compared in later analysis.

An example of this method in a rather different context is a study of pupils' levels of physical activity in secondary school Physical Education lessons (Curtner-Smith, Chen and Kerr, 1995). Forty lessons were observed using a structured system known as SOFIT (system for observing fitness instruction time) (McKenzie, Sallis and Nader, 1992). This involved coding the nature of pupil activity occurring at 20 second intervals into one of five categories – lying down, sitting, standing, walking, or 'very active', the latter being defined as 'activity that involved pupils expending more energy than during ordinary walking'. The researchers also coded at the same point in time the teachers' behaviour (into 5 categories) and the curricular context (into 4 categories). Using this method the researchers were able to estimate the percentage of lesson time pupils spent on particular activities – especially on 'very active' activities – and the percentage of time teachers devoted to different types of teaching.

A variation of time sampling was used in the STAR project mentioned above. Here researchers coded at two minute intervals whether the category of behaviour had occurred during the preceding two minutes. The advantages of this method are that a large number of behaviours or events can be recorded and some indication is gained of their minimum frequency. The problem is that the method will underestimate the frequency of behaviours which are clustered in time, and will give little information about the duration or sequencing of behaviours.

A third option is to focus recording on events. Here whenever the behaviour of interest occurs its nature, and sometimes the time at which it occurs (and less commonly its duration), is recorded. The advantage of this approach is that it gives data on the frequency of events or behaviours, and possibly on where they occur in time and sequences. However, the method does not usually give information on the duration of behaviours and will prove difficult to operate when the events of interest occur frequently in rapid succession.

An example of this type of system is the Brophy and Good Dyadic Interaction System (Brophy and Good, 1970a) which has been used for studying teacher–pupil interaction, in particular whether teachers interact differently with different categories of pupil (see, for example, Brophy and Good, 1970b). In this system the observer codes the nature of a teacher's communications to a pupil, the nature of the pupil's response, and the teacher's feedback to the pupil's response every time such events occur. So, for example, the observer codes the type of question asked of a pupil (5 categories), then the type of answer given by the pupil (5 categories), followed by the type of feedback given by the teacher to the answer (14 categories). The observer also codes pupil-initiated interactions whenever they occur.

The final decision which must be made before data collection begins is what contextual information should be recorded and how. Contextual information is obviously vital where the aim of the research is to make comparisons across contexts, but it can also be extremely important in understanding the nature of observed behaviour. What is recorded and how, as with the other decisions we have been discussing, will depend on the research questions which are being addressed.

There are varying types of contextual information that are recorded in different ways. There is routine background information that should be recorded alongside all observations, e.g. the name of the school, the date, the time, where the observations were made in the school, etc. Such information is normally noted in the headings of the observation schedule. Beyond this there is also other contextual information which is stable across the observation period and can therefore be recorded at the beginning or end of that period, e.g. certain physical features of the location, the numbers of people present, and perhaps some of their characteristics such as their gender or social position (where this is known), the basic nature of the activities going on, such as the curriculum content of a lesson or the agenda of a meeting, etc. Again this information is usually recorded in specified sections of the observation schedule.

But there is also often important contextual information which varies across the observation period. Sometimes, for example, the layout of the location may change, or the subject being observed may move, or the people with whom the subject is interacting may change, or the curriculum context of a lesson may change, and so on. Sometimes it is also important to note the behaviour of others who are not the immediate focus of the research; their behaviour can be an important context for the behaviour of the subjects under investigation, and this behavioural context is highly likely to change. In these circumstances it is usually necessary to incorporate context variables into the observation system itself. For example, as I noted above, the ORACLE observation system allowed researchers to code a number of other variables as well as pupil activity, such as the pupil's location, the teacher's activity and location, etc. These variables provided contextual information for the variable of pupil activity. It is also possible to see pupil activity as a contextual variable for some of the other behavioural categories such as the pupil's role in interaction with adults or other children. It is more feasible to include contextual variables in the observation system like this when time sampling is used, because the gaps between observations permit the coding of several different variables. It is much more difficult when observation and recording are continuous.

Another type of contextual information which is usually important to note is the observer's position and behaviour, and any information which might indicate the effect of the observer or observation on the subjects. This will be very important in judging the extent and direction of reactivity. It is usually more appropriate to record this sort of information at the end of the observation period in written form, as in field notes.

The researcher using structured observation must make decisions about all these things before data collection proper begins. These decisions are usually informed by a lengthy period of pilot work. This often involves using less structured methods to refine the research focus and develop observational categories, and trials of various recording techniques. In fact the development of an observational system which suits the purposes of the investigation can be a very lengthy exercise. This is one reason why some researchers make use of, or modify, existing systems; although care must be taken that the system chosen is appropriate for the purposes and context of the planned research. The outcome of these deliberations and decisions should be a system for recording observations which has clear rules and procedures which can be used in the same way on different occasions and by different observers.

The discussion so far has already indicated some of the advantages of this approach (see also McIntyre and Macleod, 1978). To summarize, using more structured methods 'live' is less time consuming and sometimes more practical than audio/video recording. They force the researcher to clarify the focus, and therefore the purpose, of his or her investigations, and to make explicit the methods of sampling and selection he or she has employed. They enable the collection of quantitative data, if necessary on a large scale using a team of observers, on particular pre-defined behaviours. This data permits comparisons of these behaviours between individuals, contexts and times so that patterns of similarity and difference can be identified. Moreover, the data can be analysed and related to data from other sources, such as from surveys or attainment tests, using statistical techniques. In addition the standardization of recording methods reduces the influence of the particular subjectivity of the observer. In theory all observers focus on the same behaviour, utilize the same conceptual categories, and code and record their observations in the same way. The extent to which this is achieved consistently can be checked in a number of ways. For example, two observers can observe and record the same behaviour over the same period and their recordings can be compared. This enables researchers to estimate the degree to which their methods are reliable.

Our earlier discussion has also alluded to some of the limitations of this approach (see Delamont and Hamilton, 1984). First, once a more structured observation system has been created it is, by its very nature, inflexible. Researchers cannot change the focus of their observation, the categories they employ or the way observations are recorded in response to ideas which develop or events which occur during fieldwork. Second, it has been argued that more structured recording over-simplifies a complex social reality and therefore produces inaccurate representations. It is suggested that reducing behavioural instances to tallies and codes inevitably ignores important qualitative differences and encourages observers to force behavioural instances into inadequate pre-set categories. Moreover, it is claimed that a focus on observable behaviour, without reference to the perspectives of participants and the cultural context in which they operate, means researchers often neglect subtle (and sometimes not so subtle) variations in the meaning of behaviour, and therefore fail to appreciate its true nature. These points relate to criticisms which are often made about quantitative methods in general – that, in their attempt to emulate the measurement systems of the natural sciences, they fail to capture the complex and fundamentally meaningful nature of human behaviour.

A third problem relates to the practice of more structured observational systems. The categories and rules for allocating instances to categories in some systems are rather ambiguous, and it is therefore often difficult for observers (particularly a team of observers) to code behavioural instances consistently. This particularly applies to systems which rely heavily on the observer's inference or judgement about the nature or meaning of observed behaviour.[4] Whilst such problems can be reduced by careful pilot work and effective training of observers, they do raise significant questions about the reliability of some systems.

Another practical limitation of more structured methods is that it is usually very difficult for the researcher to participate actively with the group he or she is studying. Most structured systems require the researcher's full attention to operate effectively. It is also therefore difficult for the researcher to observe covertly. These points, and the fact that observers using these methods are less likely to spend long periods in a particular observational field, mean that reactivity is more likely to be a problem.

CONCLUSION

This chapter has discussed three main methods of recording observational data – audio/video recording, field notes, and more structured techniques. We have seen that each has advantages and limitations. How then do researchers decide among them? Some researchers maintain a dogmatic attachment to particular methods. For example, some who favour ethnographic approaches often eschew more structured techniques, seeing their emphasis on the precise measurement of observable behaviour as inappropriate for the study of people. Their preference is for the detailed qualitative records provided by audio/videotapes and field notes, supplemented by data from interviews, conversations and documents. In contrast others point to the subjective and idiosyncratic nature of field notes, and stress the importance of what they see as the more rigorous, scientific approach of more structured recording. In my view dogmatic choice of this kind is unhelpful. It tends to blind researchers to the limitations of their preferred technique and to the advantages of other approaches. It therefore closes down options. I think the best strategy is to choose methods which are most suited for the particular questions under investigation, the circumstances of the research and the stage the research has reached. This sometimes means that a combination of different methods is most appropriate.

NOTES

1.   They do not give a figure for the proportion of gaze directed to neither. Their figures are based only on the parts of the video where the teacher's gaze is visible. Unfortunately, Swann and Graddol do not tell us how much this was, but point out that it was greater in the second discussion which was specifically recorded with this in mind.

2.   For a discussion of different approaches to the study of speech see Coultard, 1985, and to the study of classroom language see Edwards and Westgate, 1994.

3.   For a collection of examples of such systems see Simon and Boyer, 1970, 1974; Galton, 1978. Examples of more recently developed systems, in addition to those discussed here, can be found in Merret and Wheldall, 1986; Wragg, 1993.

4.   See Scarth and Hammersley's (1986) criticisms of the ORACLE observation system.

4

Analysing Observational Data

We saw in Chapter 3 that observation can generate three types of data – audio/video recordings and transcriptions, field notes, and the tallies produced by the use of observation schedules. These data in themselves are rarely the end product of research. Rather, they are analysed to create generalized accounts of the phenomena of concern, be it teachers' work, students' playground culture, governors' meetings, or whatever.

These accounts take three main forms – descriptions, evaluations and explanations. Producing descriptions involves combining data in order to identify the key features of, and regularities and variations in, the phenomena of interest. Producing evaluations involves comparing descriptive data with some model of how things ought, or are preferred, to be. Producing explanations involves looking for connections and relationships among data to establish the cause(s) of particular features or patterns.

These goals, and the basic features of data analysis, are the same no matter what types of data have been collected. However, the starting points and techniques used are somewhat different depending on whether the data is initially qualitative or quantitative. In this chapter I will explore some of the techniques employed, treating audio/video data and field notes as qualitative data and the tallies of more structured recording as quantitative data. Space necessitates a relatively simple level of discussion and readers requiring more detail are referred to texts dealing specifically with data analysis (for example Bryman and Crammer, 1990; Dey, 1993; Miles and Huberman, 1994). I will begin with the production of descriptions, then look briefly at evaluations, and finally consider explanations.

PRODUCING DESCRIPTIONS

Qualitative data

Before we start it is important to emphasize that data collection and analysis in qualitative research are rarely completely separate stages. They often proceed alongside each other, data being analysed shortly after it is collected, and this analysis directing further data collection. Analysis, involving the development of conceptual schemes and theoretical ideas, encourages researchers to clarify their research foci and questions, and subsequently to collect new data, or sometimes to re-analyse existing data, to shed further light on their revised research problem(s). This spiral of data collection and analysis sometimes involves the theoretical sampling which I discussed in Chapter 2.

A researcher typically begins the analysis of qualitative data by reading the data carefully in order to become thoroughly familiar with what they are about and their basic features. More importantly, the researcher begins to interrogate the data in terms of the topic of concern. The data has been collected with particular research questions in mind and the researcher must ask what the data say about these questions. He or she is also on the look out for questions which are suggested by the data itself. New ideas and avenues often emerge from a close examination of the data which can be followed up by further analysis of existing data or the collection of new data. Flexibility is particularly important in the early stages when the focus is broad and key areas of concern have yet to develop. However, there are dangers here. Foci can expand exponentially and researchers have to avoid going down too many avenues, recognizing that it is impossible to pursue every potentially interesting line of enquiry.

During this preliminary analysis the researcher is on the look out for key themes and topics, for sections of the data which seem particularly interesting, unusual or relevant, and for similarities and contrasts between different parts of the data. He or she often highlights relevant pieces of text and records his or her thoughts and ideas in the form of notes or memos. These vary from single word reminders, jotted down next to particular sections of text, to more detailed analytic memos which explore conceptual themes or potentially fruitful avenues for analysis in some detail. These notes are sometimes made in the margins next to the appropriate section of text (one reason for leaving large margins when taking field notes or transcribing tapes) or on separate sheets with their relationship to relevant parts of the data noted. Computer software designed for analysing qualitative data often has the facility to link files containing data and memos so that they can be displayed on the screen interchangeably (see Tesch, 1989; Fielding and Lee, 1991; Dey, 1993).

Another function of preliminary analysis, especially that conducted in the early stages of data collection, is the organization of the data so that it can be stored and retrieved efficiently. This is particularly important where large amounts of data are being collected on a wide variety of themes, as often happens in school case studies. In most studies audio/videotapes, transcripts and field notes are stored initially in chronological order as they are collected. But when analysis begins it is necessary to break data down into segments relating to particular topics or themes so that it can be indexed and/or stored under category headings. Initially these categories are often very broad and simple, dividing data, for example, into that which relates to particular places, people, events or times, but as the study progresses they often change, becoming narrower and more conceptually sophisticated.

Breaking down the data and organizing it in this way allows researchers to retrieve and examine all the data on particular topics, themes and categories. In the past this necessitated a good deal of time compiling indexes to the chronological record by hand, or copying, cutting and pasting pieces of data so that they could be stored in separate files. This still has to be done, but nowadays can be performed much more easily and flexibly with computer software which permits efficient cataloguing and indexing, and rapid copying, searching and retrieval of data – that is if one is prepared to invest the time learning to use the software and inputting the data.

The second stage in the analysis of qualitative data involves the development of conceptual categories with which the data can be classified. Conceptual categories are simply labels assigned to types of phenomena sharing certain characteristics. The labels symbolize these shared characteristics. Organizing the data into categories reduces its complexity and highlights the important features of the phenomena under study. Beynon (1985), for example, during his study of initial encounters between teachers and first year boys in a single-sex comprehensive school became interested in the strategies used by boys to type or 'sus-out' their teachers. He focused on behaviour which appeared to have this function and found that it could be divided into 6 main categories – 'group formation and communication', 'joking', 'challenging actions (verbal)', 'challenges (non-verbal)', 'interventions', and 'play'. He refined these categories to form several sub-categories. For example, he distinguished between 'open joking' and 'covert joking', and divided the former into 5 categories – 'jokes based on pupils' 'names', 'risque jokes', 'lavatorial humour', 'repartee and wit' and 'set pieces'.

Ideas for category systems come from a number of sources. Sometimes the research questions relate to existing conceptual schemes and may suggest or precipitate categories. For example, researchers on the Oxford Preschool Project (Sylva, Roy and Painter, 1986) were concerned to identify the different types of activities that children engaged in in playgroups and nursery schools. On the basis of existing knowledge, and through close examination of their observational data (which took the form of detailed field notes), they developed a set of 30 activity categories which described what they felt were the key features of the children's activities. These included things like – 'gross motor play: active movement requiring coordination of larger muscles', 'large scale construction: arranging and building dens, trains and so on, with large crates or boxes', and 'rough-and-tumble: informal, spontaneous play involving body movement in social interaction' (pp. 31–5).

Sometimes more novel categories may spring from the data itself. Detailed scrutiny of it can suggest new categories which highlight important features of the phenomena under study not previously recognized. For example, Hargreaves (1981) when studying teacher talk during curriculum development meetings developed the categories of 'contrastive rhetoric' and 'extremist talk' to describe the ways in which teachers discussed the possibility of radical educational innovation. 'Contrastive rhetoric' referred to talk which discouraged such innovation by trivializing and negatively stereotyping alternatives to current practice. In contrast 'extremist talk' was a way in which a small number of teachers introduced radical ideas and challenged the boundaries of normal practice.

Whatever the source of ideas for category systems it is important that categories are relevant to the questions which the research is addressing. It is also important that they are not imposed on the data, but reflect real distinctions – that they are 'grounded' (Glaser and Strauss, 1967) in the data. This does not imply that the distinctions must be immediately apparent, but it does require that categories are developed through the close examination of the data. Involved here is a continual process of comparing pieces of data and identifying the relevant similarities and differences among them. What is regarded as a piece of data depends, of course, on the focus of the research, the questions it addresses, and the stage or level of analysis reached. If the focus is, for example, on the linguistic features of interaction then a piece of data can be as small as one word (or even one sound). On the other hand if the focus is on, say, broad teacher strategies the description of a whole lesson may constitute the relevant unit of data.

Glaser and Strauss (1967) refer to the process of comparing pieces of data as 'the constant comparative method'. They explain that comparison allows the researcher to establish the range of particular categories and the variation within categories. In other words it enables him or her to clarify what pieces of data can be allocated to particular categories by developing the defining characteristics of the categories and the criteria by which data can be allocated to them. Using the example of Hargreaves' (1981) work, comparison enabled him to decide what instances of teacher talk could be categorized as referring to radical innovation and within this what instances could be categorized as contrastive rhetoric and what as extremist talk.[1]

This process also involves clarifying the relationships among categories. Categories can be hierarchically related, referring to different levels of detail in the data.This can be seen in Beynon's (1985) system where types of joking are clearly sub-types of a category at a higher level of abstraction – a sussing-out strategy. The higher level category here is inclusive of the lower level ones, which means a piece of data belongs under both headings.

Categories at the same level can be either inclusive or exclusive (Dey, 1993). They are often inclusive when distinctions are made between them on a number of different criteria. In these circumstances a piece of data can be placed in more than one category depending on the criteria used. Some of Beynon's joking categories, for example, appear to be inclusive – 'lavatorial humour' and 'repartee and wit', for example. Here he appears to make distinctions between instances of joking on the basis of the content of jokes and on the speed of their delivery, so that it might be possible to place a particular instance in both categories. With exclusive categories we should only be able to allocate a piece of data to one or other category. Hargreaves' (1981) categories of 'contrastive rhetoric' and 'extremist talk', for example, seem to be exclusive. A key difference is that in the former radical educational innovation is viewed negatively, whereas in the latter it is viewed positively.

One problem with much qualitative research is that the defining characteristics of categories and the relationships among them are not clearly specified. This is certainly the case with Beynon's work. It is unclear, for example, how he defined pupils' 'sussing-out strategies' and distinguished them from other pupil strategies, and many of his types and sub-types of strategy are also ambiguous and poorly differentiated. This can become a particular problem where the researcher wishes to quantify the data allocated to different categories.

Comparison often results in the extension of category systems in various directions. The development of some categories may suggest others at the same level. These categories may not always be apparent in the data, but may be logically implied given the conceptual distinctions which are being made. In the Oxford Preschool Project (Sylva, Roy and Painter, 1986), for example, the activity category 'large scale construction' implied the existence of another category 'small scale construction' which was incorporated in the conceptual scheme of children's activities. Categories can thus extend horizontally until all relevant ones have been identified. Relevant distinctions can also be made within categories resulting in their division into sub-categories, as we have seen in the case of Beynon's (1985) research. Comparison can also suggest similarities between categories at a higher level of conceptualization. For example, types of student behaviour might be grouped together in terms of whether they indicated a pro- or anti-school disposition on the part of certain students.

A lot of qualitative research does not go much further than the development of category systems which describe relevant distinctions in the data and highlight what the researcher sees as the key features of the phenomena under investigation. But sometimes comparison of the data allocated to different categories reveals interesting variations and patterns. For example, in studying the data on different types of children's play a researcher might discover that some types of play occur more frequently than others (or, if the duration of particular instances was recorded, that some types of play take up more time than others). Clearly what is involved here is the counting of instances of children's play allocated to particular categories and comparison of the quantitative differences between categories.

The researcher might also notice that instances of play allocated to particular categories are more likely to involve certain types of children or happen at certain times or follow certain other activities. Here what is being noted is that the instances of children's play allocated to the play categories are more or less likely to fall into other categories. These categories are contextual, relating, for example, to the social group of the subject, or the time the behaviour occurred, or its geographical location, or its sequential location in respect of other behaviours, and so on. In other words what the researcher notes is a quantitative relationship between the different ways in which instances have been categorized. These patterns can be represented by cross-tabulating data allocated to different categories. This is illustrated in Table 4.1 with some fictitious data for children's play which shows a variation on gender lines. Exploring these sorts of patterns in the data obviously involves the translation of qualitative data into quantitative forms. In this way it is possible to see quantitative analysis as an extension of qualitative analysis – in a sense as beginning where much qualitative analysis ends.[2]

Table 4.1 Incidence of children's play categories by gender

	Gross motor play	Large scale construction	Smale scale construction	Art	Pretend	Total
Boys	20	35	46	12	17	130
Girls	15	23	25	38	41	142
Total	35	58	71	50	58	272

Categories derived from Sylva, Roy and Painter (1986).

Quantitative data

Quantitative observational data consist of tallies or codes which indicate that a particular category of behaviour was observed.[3] Where the data collected were originally qualitative the tallies and codes will often be annotated to field notes, transcripts or to pieces of data selected from the main text. Where behaviour was coded at the point of observation the tallies or codes will usually be recorded on some sort of standardized observation schedule designed for the purpose. Also normally recorded and coded will be data about the people involved – most importantly their name or social category – and contextual data concerning the temporal, physical and social context in which the observed behaviour occurred.

For the purpose of analysis it is possible to see these data in the same way as the survey researcher conceives of his or her respondents' answers to structured interview questions. In a survey each respondent is seen as a case, and his or her answers are seen as fitting into the categories of different variables. With observational data each observation can be seen as a case which then is placed into categories on a number of variables. Data can be displayed in the form of a matrix in which rows represent observations (the cases) and columns the variables. In a project employing the Flanders Interaction Analysis system, for example, we might see the data as in Table 4.2. (Again this data is fictitious.)

Table 4.2 Data displayed in a matrix

Cases	Variables				
	Flanders Cats.	Teacher I.D.	Lesson No.	Subject Code	Pupil Year Group
Observation 1	4	3	6	2	9
Observation 2	4	3	6	2	9
Observation 3	8	3	6	2	9
Observation 4	10	3	6	2	9
Observation 5	5	3	6	2	9
Observation 6	5	3	6	2	9

Here we have data on six observations (or cases), and, as the Flanders categories are coded every three seconds, they relate to only 18 seconds of observation time. A project involving 10 hours of observation time would therefore generate 12,000 observations/cases. The only behavioural variable coded is teacher–pupil interaction and the numbers in this column refer to the 10 categories of this variable (see Figure 1.1). The other variables are contextual and the codes here remain the same as long as the observations refer to the same teacher, lesson, subject and pupil year group. This is a relatively simple example with only one behavioural variable. In a project like ORACLE (Galton, Simon and Croll, 1980) where several behavioural variables were coded simultaneously there would be a much larger number of columns, though fewer rows for the same amount of observation time, as observations in this project were recorded at 25 second intervals.

Often with observational data the variables involved are nominal. In other words they are simply divided into two or more categories that cannot be ranked. Teacher–pupil interaction in the Flanders system is a nominal variable with 10 categories, as are variables like gender, curriculum subject, whether a pupil is on or off task, and so on. Sometimes variables are ordinal which means that the categories can be ranked in terms of more or less of a particular variable. An observational rating in which the quality of teaching was judged poor, satisfactory, good, or very good, is an example. Here we can say that good is a higher category than satisfactory, though we cannot say that the difference between very good and good is the same as between good and satisfactory. In other words the intervals between the ranks cannot be specified. The other main types of variable are interval and ratio variables. Here the categories can be ranked, the differences between the categories are numerically the same, and, for ratio variables, there is a fixed zero point. At the level of individual observations behavioural variables are rarely interval or ratio, but contextual variables sometimes are. Examples include chronological age, IQ, examination scores, and so on. It is possible to employ a wider variety of statistical tests in analysing interval and ratio variables. Indeed, these distinctions between types of variables are important because the statistical procedures which can be used depend on the nature of the variables that are the focus of the research.

Quantitative data from individual observations can be summarized by simply counting the number of times, or calculating the length of time, a particular category was coded. In the example of the Flanders Interaction Analysis data given above the researcher would count the number of times each interaction category was coded over a particular period. What is important here is the unit of analysis (Croll, 1986) across which these calculations are made. This depends on the focus of the research. Sometimes the researcher may wish to compare individual teachers or pupils or social categories of teachers or pupils, in which case he or she will combine all observations relating to such individuals or groups, working out, for example, how many times, or for how long, teacher A's or pupil B's behaviour is coded in a particular way. In other cases researchers may be concerned with how often or how long a particular category of behaviour is coded in a certain time unit. Here the unit of analysis may be lessons, or a particular activity within lessons or a whole day, and all observations relating to that time unit are included in the calculations. Another possibility is how often or how long particular categories of behaviour occur within a physical or institutional unit such as a department or a school.

In effect what is being done here is that the behaviour code allocated to a particular instance is related to various contextual codings. So (as we noted above with qualitative data) the researcher will count the number of times a particular behavioural code is allocated to instances which have also been allocated certain contextual codes. Let me illustrate this with some further fictitious data employing the Flanders categories. In Table 4.3 all the observational instances coded in the Flanders categories relating to teacher A have been counted, all those relating to teacher B, and so on. And what we have is a series of frequency distributions for the different teachers which can be displayed as a cross-tabulation.

Table 4.3 Data on 4 teachers derived from approx. 30 minutes of observation using the Flanders Interaction Analysis System

Cases	Variables: Flanders Interaction Analysis Categories										Total no. of obs.
	1	2	3	4	5	6	7	8	9	10	
Teacher A	20 (3)	25 (4)	31 (5)	63 (10)	131 (22)	95 (16)	104 (18)	54 (9)	23 (4)	54 (9)	600 (100)
Teacher B	20 (3)	46 (6)	30 (4)	96 (13)	140 (19)	135 (18)	42 (5)	90 (12)	84 (11)	67 (9)	750 (100)
Teacher C	10 (2)	23 (5)	40 (8)	84 (17)	67 (13)	72 (14)	23 (5)	76 (15)	70 (14)	35 (7)	500 (100)
Teacher D	37 (6)	76 (12)	100 (16)	96 (14)	52 (8)	40 (6)	21 (3)	109 (17)	76 (11)	46 (7)	650 (100)

Figures in brackets are percentages

Another way of combining these data might be to relate instances coded in the Flanders categories to say the teachers' subject departments. If teachers A and B are in the maths department and teachers C and D in the English department we would get the information displayed in Table 4.4. As I have suggested, other possibilities might be to combine observational instances related to particular person categories, locational categories, or other institutional categories, etc. What happens here is that certain contextual categories, rather than individual observations, become the units of analysis and the data related to them are combined and compared. It is important to realize that when we do this the nature of cases and variables changes. In Table 4.3 the teachers become the cases and in Table 4.4 the departments are the

Table 4.4 Relating data to teachers' subject departments

	Variables: Flanders Interaction Analysis Categories										Total no. of obs.
	1	2	3	4	5	6	7	8	9	10	
Maths teachers	40 (3)	71 (5)	61 (4)	159 (12)	271 (20)	230 (17)	146 (11)	144 (11)	107 (8)	121 (9)	1350 (100)
English teachers	47 (4)	99 (8)	140 (12)	178 (16)	119 (10)	112 (10)	44 (4)	185 (16)	146 (13)	81 (7)	1150 (100)

Figures in brackets are percentages

cases. In both tables the observational categories themselves become variables of a ratio type. Thus each teacher, or department, now has a score on each of the observational categories.

Sometimes the frequency distributions resulting from these calculations present only the actual numbers of observations. More often, in order to facilitate comparisons, these are related to some baseline by the use of proportions or percentages. The researcher works out what proportion or percentage of all observations across a particular unit of analysis were coded in a particular way. I have added this information in brackets in Tables 4.3 and 4.4 and this allows a more valid comparison of the teachers (or departments) to be made since the total number of observations recorded on each teacher is different. We can now say, for example, that 22 per cent of observations of teacher A were coded category 5 – in other words that an estimated 22 per cent of teacher A's time across the observation period was spent 'lecturing', whereas only 8 per cent of teacher D's time was spent in this way. This type of data can also, of course, be presented graphically in the form of bar charts, histograms and pie charts, where this is appropriate.

Where variables are at the interval/ratio level, data on a number of cases can be summarized using measures of central tendency or averages. The most commonly used is the arithmetic mean calculated by adding the scores on all the cases and dividing by the number of cases. For example, in a study of 10 teachers we might be interested in the average proportion of time that each spent on questioning (category 4 of the Flanders system) in which case we could add up each teacher's score on this variable and divide by 10. Other measures of central tendency are the median – the middle score of a range of cases, and the mode – the score that occurs most frequently (though where there are only two cases as in Table 4.4 medians and modes are inapplicable).

Measures of central tendency give typical or representative scores for a number of cases on a particular variable. Also of interest sometimes is the amount of variation in the distribution of scores – the degree to which the scores are spread out – information which is concealed by averages. For example, we may want to know whether all the 10 teachers are similar in the proportion of time they spend on questioning or whether there is a large variation among them. There are a number of measures of dispersion which can be used here. The simplest is the range, which is the difference between the highest and lowest score. The most commonly used is the standard deviation which is basically the average amount of deviation from the mean of all the scores in a distribution.[4]

In small scale projects these sorts of calculations can be worked out with paper, pencil and a simple calculator. However, on larger projects it is usually necessary to employ computers. A number of software packages are available for handling quantitative data, but by far the most commonly used is SPSS (Statistical Package for the Social Sciences) which is available on mainframe computers (SPSS-X) or for personal computers (SPSS-PC) (see Cramer, 1994). It is necessary to input the data into the computer in the form of a matrix (like the ones we have already looked at) consisting of a large number of rows and a more limited number (usually up to about eighty) columns. The rows consist of the data on individual cases and the columns the data on individual variables.

An important question with observational data is what constitutes the cases and variables. As I have explained already, it is possible to see each observation as a case and observational and contextual categories as the variables; here the individual observation is the unit of analysis. However, where a project involves a large number of observations it will be impractical to input data in this form – there will simply be far too many cases. It is more sensible therefore to input data at a higher unit of analysis, seeing, for example, subjects (or categories of subject), or time periods, or institutional units as the cases. This clearly involves combining some of the 'raw' data and entering them in a composite form which results in some loss of detail.

Once the data has been entered and stored in an appropriate data file, various commands, depending on the software being used, can be given to enable the computer to conduct the sorts of descriptive statistical analyses which we have already discussed, and the more complex analyses we will discuss shortly.

PRODUCING EVALUATIONS

The process of analysis to produce evaluations does not differ significantly from that involved in producing descriptions. Where the comparison between how a phenomenon ought, or is preferred, to be and how it is observed to be occurs at the point of data collection, the raw data in effect consists of a large number of descriptions in terms of the evaluative criteria. These can be in the form of quantitative ratings – as is the case in school inspections – or qualitative accounts – such as might occur where a teacher evaluates the classroom performance of a colleague. Analysis in this situation involves combining the data in the same ways as other qualitative and quantitative data to identify key areas of strength and weakness (from the observer's point of view) and significant similarities and variations in their distribution.

Where the comparison of ideal and reality occurs after data collection the ideal model often becomes the guiding focus of analysis. The researcher will sift and sort his or her data to produce a descriptive account of how things are observed to be in terms of the key aspects of his or her model of how they should be. Account and model are compared, and key areas and patterns of strength and weakness are identified. This was the approach I adopted in my own research in a multi-ethnic school which I have referred to in earlier chapters (Foster, 1990a). One of my aims was to discover whether the teachers had succeeded in creating a non-racist environment in the school, in which pupils of all ethnic groups were treated equitably. I therefore first specified an ideal model of such an environment, clarifying what I felt was meant by equitable treatment. This model became the focus of my analysis which involved exploring the data I had collected to see to what extent the reality I observed was congruent with, or diverged from, my ideal.

The same basic process is involved in much action research. Here relevant observational data are selected and combined to produce a description of current practice, which is then compared with key aspects of an ideal model to identify areas of congruence or incongruence. Similarly, in much research on educational innovation what is observed where the innovation is introduced is compared with what is observed where it is not, and this information is used to make judgements about the efficacy of the innovation.

Again in these situations the techniques of data analysis are the same as those outlined above; the only difference is that key features of the ideal, or preferred, model provide the evaluative criteria on which the analysis proceeds.

PRODUCING EXPLANATIONS

Producing explanations involves trying to discover why some descriptive or evaluative feature or pattern in a phenomenon exists. Swann and Graddol (1988), for example, whose research I discussed in Chapter 3, were not only concerned to describe the gender differences in pupil participation in class discussions they observed, but also to discover what caused these to occur.

Observational data can be used in two ways in producing explanations. First, a pattern revealed in the observational data can be the phenomenon to be explained. Sometimes researchers are concerned to explore the causes of qualitative patterns; in other words to discover why instances of observed behaviour have the characteristics they do. Woods (1979), for example, wanted to explain why teachers adopted survival strategies, and why these took the particular forms they did. At other times researchers attempt to explain quantitative patterns. They wish to explore why particular categories of behaviour occur more frequently (or for longer) than other categories or why they occur more often amongst certain subjects or situations. So Swann and Graddol (1988), for example, wanted to explain why boys had *more* interactional turns than girls. Used in this way the patterns revealed in observational data are the effects of factors which are to be discovered. In the language of quantitative research they are dependent variables.

The second way observational data can be used is in relation to explanatory variables. For instance, observational data on teacher behaviour might be used to explain patterns of pupil achievement or attitudes. Green (1983), for example, used observational data on interaction patterns in the classrooms of a number of primary and middle school teachers to explain ethnic group differences in pupils' self-esteem.[5] Similarly, observational data on pupils could be used to explain patterns in teachers' behaviour, attitudes or dispositions. In my own work (Foster, 1990a), for example, I argued that some of the characteristics of the teacher behaviour I observed (which was similar in many respects to the behaviour Woods (1979) observed) were, in part at least, the product of the negative and disruptive behaviour of many pupils (though this explanation remained rather implicit in my work). Used in this way the categorized as challenging to see whether the same precipitating features were present there.

If this examination of the data revealed that instances of challenging behaviour commonly involve boys, but not girls, and that instances of conformist behaviour more frequently involve girls than boys, then there would seem to be a possibility of a causal link between challenging/conformist behaviour and the child's sex (or more likely gender). If the examination also shows that challenging behaviour happens often during maths lessons, but conformist behaviour is more likely during other subject lessons, then there seems to be a possible causal link between maths lessons and challenging/conformist behaviour. We seem to have discovered two potentially causal factors here. These relationships can be illustrated by simple cross-tabulations as in Tables 4.5 and 4.6.

Table 4.5 Incidence of challenging and conformist behaviour by sex of child

	Boys	Girls
Challenging behaviour	high	low
Conformist behaviour	low	high

Table 4.6 Incidence of challenging and conformist behaviour in maths and other subject lessons

	In maths lessons	In other subject lessons
Challenging behaviour	high	low
Conformist behaviour	low	high

Let me give another illustration of this process, this time using a published piece of research. In a study of teacher–student interaction in a multi-ethnic comprehensive school Gillborn (1990) argues that the teachers tended to respond negatively to the culturally based behaviour of many Afro-Caribbean students. He explains this pattern of behaviour by reference to the teachers' ethnocentric attitudes. The teachers' attitudes, he claims, caused them to behave negatively towards the students' behaviour.

In order to establish this explanation Gillborn needed to examine all instances in his data of negative teacher response to Afro-Caribbean students' culturally based behaviour which he categorized and to examine the attitudes of the teachers involved to see if they were ethnocentric. He also needed to examine instances of teacher response not categorized as negative and the attitudes of the teachers involved in these cases. His explanation would have some substance if what he found from this process of comparison was that teachers involved in negative responses had ethnocentric attitudes, whereas those involved in non-negative responses did not; or, put another way, if teachers with ethnocentric attitudes tended to respond negatively whereas patterns in observational data are the causal factors, the independent var, which explain the existence of other phenomena.

Hammersley and Atkinson (1995) point out that there is only one me for developing explanations – the comparative method, and the 'pu version of this is the experiment. As I explained in Chapter 2, in its basic fo this involves comparing the impact of different treatments on similar ca while all other relevant factors are held constant. In this way it is possible say, with more confidence than with other methods, that any difference in th two cases recorded after treatments was *caused by* the difference in treatment.

Whilst experimental research is sometimes conducted in schools, fo practical and ethical reasons school research which develops explanations is much more likely to involve the comparison of data collected on naturally occurring cases. As with description, the basic process of analysis is the same whether the data is qualitative or quantitative, but there are some differences in the techniques employed.

Qualitative data

The process by which researchers search for explanations using qualitative data is often not made explicit, but the most common approach involves taking further the comparison between instances we discussed earlier. Typically the researcher tries to discover links between the different ways in which pieces of data can be categorized. He or she examines carefully all pieces of data allocated to a category and searches for precipitating features which the pieces might share. Such features might be the social or cultural context in which behaviour occurred, or the perspectives, attitudes or motives of the subject(s), or the physical or temporal location of the subject(s). At the same time the researcher will examine instances of data allocated to other categories to see if the same precipitating features are present or absent in these instances. If a particular feature is found to coincide frequently with the instances being explained and not with others then the chances of it being a causal factor increase.[6]

Let me illustrate this process with a simple fictitious example. Supposing in a study of pupils' classroom behaviour we found that some instances of behaviour could be described as challenging classroom norms whereas others could be categorized as more conformist. To search for explanations for this pattern we could examine all instances of behaviour categorized as challenging and look for precipitating features which these instances might have in common. We might look at the characteristics of the actors involved – their age, sex, intelligence, for example. We might also explore the views and perspectives of those involved. We could also consider the physical, social and temporal context in which their behaviour occurred. Let us say we found that many instances of challenging behaviour involved boys and that they were more likely to occur at particular times, in fact during maths lessons. At the same time we could also examine all instances of pupils' behaviour not those with non-ethnocentric attitudes did not. Unfortunately, it is not clear whether Gillborn conducted this sort of comparative analysis, and this casts some doubt on the credibility of his explanatory claims. However, Gillborn is not alone here. A weakness of much qualitative research in education (and other areas) is that explanations are not adequately tested.

Something which is important to recognize is that the searches for explanatory factors which I have outlined in these two examples are not conducted blind. They are generally directed by some sort of existing theory, although often this theory is not clearly articulated. The fact that we looked to see whether or not there was a link between challenging/conformist behaviour and pupils' sex was because we anticipated there might be such a connection. This idea derived from our existing theoretical knowledge about the relationship between people's sex and their behaviour. Similarly, looking for a possible link between challenging/conformist behaviour and the subject of lessons was probably induced by the idea that there could be some plausible connection between the two.

These theories often precede the research itself. In fact, although it is claimed that a characteristic feature of qualitative research is that researchers minimize the influence of preconceived ideas, in many cases such ideas are the main driving force behind their work, influencing to a considerable extent the explanatory factors they choose to explore. At the same time in many projects theoretical ideas emerge during the course of the research, and analysis involves exploring the data in order to test them. In fact these theoretical ideas sometimes become the basis for data collection through the process of theoretical sampling which I described in Chapter 2.

As I also pointed out in Chapter 2, a lot of qualitative research in education consists of case studies of particular schools or even of groups of teachers and pupils within schools. Our discussion so far has focused on how researchers search for explanations by making comparisons between pieces of data from *within* the case studied. Another possible source of comparison is *between* cases. In many qualitative studies this goes on implicitly. Woods (1979), for example, explains the fact that teachers in the school he studied utilized survival strategies by reference to certain contextual features of the environment in which the teachers were forced to work. Implicit here is the suggestion that in schools where such features were absent teachers would not, or would be less likely to, use survival strategies.

The substantiation of Woods' theory that teacher survival strategies were caused by certain features of teachers' work environment would require comparisons between schools. Either schools which differ in terms of their relevant contextual features could be compared to see whether their teachers were more or less likely to employ survival strategies, or schools where teachers utilize or do not utilize survival strategies could be compared to see whether their contextual features differed in the expected way. In fact a number of schools might be selected here as critical cases (see Chapter 2). Unfortunately, as Hammersley (1985) points out, very little qualitative research has been organized with this sort of theory testing in mind. One exception he notes is the work by Hargreaves (1967), Lacey (1970) and Ball (1981),[7] which can be seen as a series of school case studies orientated to developing and testing the theory that the differentiation of pupils on academic and behavioural lines causes their attitudes to school to polarize. Another exception is Hammersley's own work with Scarth (Hammersley and Scarth, 1986) which I mentioned in Chapter 2. This research explored the theory that difference in the mode of assessment on courses in the same school subjects was a factor in determining the style of teaching which was adopted.

This discussion highlights that searching for explanations requires the comparison of cases – whether these cases are individual observations, subjects, institutional units or institutions themselves – and looking for relationships between the different ways in which cases are categorized. Of course, discovering the sorts of relationship we have discussed so far does not necessarily mean that we have uncovered causal links. To be more certain about this (and we can never be absolutely certain) analysis needs to take account of a number of other conditions.

First, the researcher must check that there is a chronology – a temporal sequence – in the relationship which has been discovered. Clearly for something to cause something else it must precede it in time. In the examples we have discussed so far there seems little doubt about this. For instance, in my fictitious example pupils' sex obviously precedes their classroom behaviour, as does their presence in maths lessons. Similarly in Woods' (1979) research there seems to be a temporal sequence in the conditions in which teachers work and their adoption of particular classroom strategies. However, establishing chronology is not always straightforward. For example, supposing we discovered a relationship between a teacher's behaviour and the attitudes of pupils to the teacher, such that negative teacher behaviour tended to be found with negative pupil attitudes. One possible chronological sequence is that the teacher's behaviour preceded the pupils' attitudes, suggesting that the teacher's behaviour causes the attitudes. But, equally, it may be that pupil attitudes come before teacher behaviour, implying a reverse causal link. More likely still is that there is a complex interactive effect here in which both phenomena cause, and are caused by, each other over time.

A second condition which must be explored is the theoretical plausibility of a causal link. The likelihood that a relationship between one type of event and another is causal is considerably enhanced if such a link is plausible – in other words if our existing knowledge suggests that there is a strong possibility of such a link and also what the nature of that link might be. Looking again at my fictitious example, a causal link between pupils' sex and the extent to which their behaviour is challenging or conformist has some plausibility given what we know about sex differences in human behaviour. On the other hand, a link between maths lessons and the nature of pupil behaviour seems less plausible. I can build a speculative theory here – that perhaps pupils find maths more difficult than other subjects and therefore tend to behave more disruptively.

But this theory is not well established, and I am therefore less inclined to accept that the relationship I discovered was causal.

A third condition which analysis needs to address is the possibility that the phenomenon was caused by other factors. For example, it might be the case that the apparent relationship between maths lessons and challenging/conformist behaviour is in fact caused by differences between the teaching methods of the maths and other subject teachers. Perhaps the maths teachers tend to be more liberal in the classroom, the pupils perceive them as 'soft', and they take advantage by being more challenging and less conformist. Thus maybe it is not the nature of maths as a subject which causes the variation in the children's behaviour, as we originally thought, but differences in the teachers' approach to classroom discipline.

In analysing the data researchers have to be alert to the possibility of alternative explanations like this. Indeed, they should actively explore them, because if they can be ruled out the strength of any explanation put forward is enhanced. Much is to be gained here by searching the data for disconfirming cases, i.e. cases which do not seem to fit an emerging explanation. For example, we might examine instances of challenging behaviour which do not occur in maths lessons (or instances of conformist behaviour which occur in them), asking what possible precipitating features these instances have in common and what alternative explanatory avenues they suggest.

Quantitative data

Searching for explanations with quantitative data involves basically the same processes of comparison of cases, but this time employing statistical techniques. I do not intend to go into the detail of these techniques. For this readers should consult basic texts on statistics – for example Cramer (1994). This discussion will be restricted to basic principles.

At its simplest in looking for explanations the researcher compares the frequency with which cases are allocated to different categories of variables on which data has been collected, searching for co-variation. Often a co-variation between two variables is expected on the basis of an existing theory (indeed, this theory may have dictated the type of data which was collected), or more specifically a hypothesis, and the researcher examines the data to see if his or her hypothesis can be accepted or rejected.

Let us take a very straightforward example. Supposing in a study of pupils' classroom behaviour we were interested in whether there was a relationship between pupils' sex and whether they were on- or off-task. Treating individual observations as our cases (or units of analysis) we discover the pattern of data shown in Table 4.7. Here each observation is allocated to one of the two categories on the task variable and one of the two on the gender variable, and it is easy to see at a glance from the cross-tabulation that there is a relationship – girls are more likely to be on-task than boys, and boys are more likely to be off-task than girls.

Table 4.7   Pupils' on- or off-task behaviour by gender

	On-task	Off-task	Total
Boys	15	35	50
Girls	41	9	50
Total	56	44	100

There is essentially no difference between this procedure and the one outlined earlier for qualitative data. With quantitative data, however, researchers usually go a stage further and check the reliability of their conclusions by using statistical tests. A researcher would be interested here in how likely it was that the relationship in the data occurred by chance. To answer this he or she would probably use a chi-squared test. This test basically compares (by subtraction) the observed figures in the data with those which would be expected if there were no relationship between the variables (i.e. if the figures in all the cells in Table 4.7 were 25). It tests what is referred to as the null hypothesis – the proposition that there is no relationship between pupils' sex and their on- or off-task behaviour. The greater the difference between observed and expected frequencies the higher is the value of chi-square. The resulting value of chi-square (26.44 for Table 4.7) is looked up in a 'table of critical values' which tells us the probability (p) that our figures occurred by chance. A low probability (e.g. $p < 0.01$ – in other words the figures in our data would have occurred by chance less than once in 100 times) – would lead the researcher to conclude that the relationship in the data is statistically significant (to reject the null hypothesis), whereas a high probability would lead him/her to conclude that it was statistically insignificant – in other words too likely to be a chance occurrence (the null hypothesis would be accepted). What level of significance is set depends on the risk of error the researcher is prepared to accept. For Table 4.7 the value of chi-square is well above that normally required to conclude that the relationship is statistically significant (in fact $p < 0.001$).

Cross-tabulations and testing for statistical significance like this are the basic ways in which researchers explore relationships among data on two different variables (often called bi-variate analysis). Sometimes, of course, subjects, rather than observations, are seen as the cases and variables are at the ordinal, interval or ratio level. For example, in a study exploring the relationship between the type of teaching used in science lessons and pupil achievement we might compare teachers categorized in terms of the proportion of their lessons given to direct instruction, and in terms of the mean achievement of their pupils on a science test. The result might be the data shown in Table 4.8.

Here raw scores on each of the two ratio level variables for individual teachers have been grouped into three ordinal level categories to enable a simpler display of the data in a 9 cell cross-tabulation. Looking at the table we can see that there does seem to be a relationship between the level of class time taken up by direct instruction and the level of pupils' mean achievement. But

Table 4.8 Mean class scores on science test by proportion of lesson time teachers spend on direct instruction. Figures in brackets are row percentages

Level of Direct Instruction	Mean class scores 70+	40–69	Below 40	Total
20%+	24 (53)	15 (33)	6 (13)	45 (100)
10–19%	12 (31)	9 (23)	18 (46)	39 (100)
Below 10%	7 (19)	8 (21)	22 (60)	37 (100)
Total	43	32	46	121

again we would want to check whether this was statistically significant using chi-square. The value of chi-square here is 24.8 which means the relationship is statistically significant ($p < 0.01$). This, of course, does not establish that there is a causal relationship, but it does provide important evidence.

Another possibility is that one variable is at the nominal level whilst the other is at the interval/ratio level. This is common in experimental designs where the research tries to measure the impact of two different treatments on similar groups. Supposing, for instance, that a school wished to test the effectiveness of new procedures designed to reduce the amount of disruptive behaviour during lessons. It might apply the new procedures to one half of a year group, but not to the other (thus producing an experimental group and a control group) and measure the number of disruptive incidents which occur subsequently in a sample of lessons for each half year. Here lessons would be the cases and each lesson would be coded into one of two categories on the 'procedures' variable – new procedures or existing procedures (the independent variable), and given a score for the number of disruptive incidents (the dependent variable). The disruptive incidents variable could be collapsed into an ordinal level variable (as in our last example), but more appropriate here would be to calculate the mean number of disruptive incidents for each category of the independent variable (though we would also need to look at the variation). A statistical test, in this case probably a t-test, would then be used to discover whether the difference between the two means was statistically significant.

Whether a relationship is statistically significant is the first thing researchers want to know. But they may also be interested in knowing the strength and direction of any relationship. To discover this researchers employ statistical techniques which measure the strength of the *correlation* between two variables. The measures are referred to as correlation coefficients. The particular coefficient used will depend on the type of data (see Bryman and Cramer, 1990, p. 187). For example, where the data is on two dichotomous variables (as in Table 4.7) the coefficient phi is used, whereas if the data is on two interval variables (as it would be employing the original data used to compile Table 4.8) then the appropriate coefficient is Pearson's *r*. The possible values of a correlation coefficient usually vary between −1 and +1. Values towards +1 indicate a strong positive relationship, i.e. as one variable increases so does the other one; values towards –1 indicate a strong negative relationship, i.e. as one variable increases the other decreases; values towards 0 indicate a weak or non-existent relationship.

Correlation coefficients are sometimes converted into percentages (by squaring them and multiplying by 100). These figures tell us how far the variation on one variable is accounted for by variation in another. For example, if we found a correlation of +0.7 between pupils' achievement scores and the length of time they spent interacting with the teacher we could say that 49 per cent of the variation in the pupils' scores was accounted for by the variation in the time spent with the teacher. But care is needed here because we can also say that 49 per cent of the variation in the time spent with the teacher is accounted for by variation in pupils' achievement scores. This highlights the important point that correlation is not synonymous with causation. A correlation tells us the strength of a statistical relationship. To decide whether this relationship is causal, and moreover which variable causes which, we must follow the procedures outlined above in connection with qualitative data.

For ratio and interval variables correlations are sometimes graphically represented in the form of scattergrams. These graphs plot each case in the data against their respective value on the two variables. For example, we might plot pupils in terms of their achievement scores and the amount of lesson time they spent interacting with the teacher. Data for 20 pupils is shown in Figure 4.1. Scattergrams like this allow the researcher to see at a glance whether there is a relationship between the variables, how strong it is, what direction it is in and whether it is linear or non-linear.

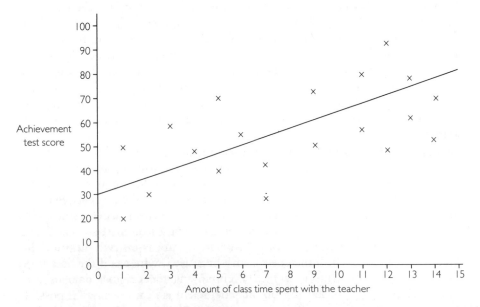

Figure 4.1   Scattergram showing data for 20 pupils

They also facilitate a technique called regression analysis. This involves summarizing the relationship between two variables with a straight line on the scattergram. This is called the 'line of best fit' and is the line from which points on the scattergram deviate least. The position and slope of the line can be expressed as a simple equation:

$$y = a + bx$$

where y and x are the dependent and independent variables respectively, a is the point of intersection of the line on the y axis, and b is the slope of the line or the regression coefficient. This enables us to say how much one variable changes (usually the dependent variable) for each unit of change in the other (usually the independent variable), and to predict the likely value of one variable from given values of the other. For example, from the data in Figure 4.1 we can say that for a 1 unit increase in the amount of time spent with the teacher we can expect an increase in achievement score of 3.33; and where a pupil spends 12 units of lesson time with the teacher his or her likely achievement score will be 70.

The discussion so far has concerned relationships between two variables. Researchers are sometimes interested in relationships among three or more variables. Their work here is often referred to as multivariate analysis. There are a number of possibilities.

First, a researcher may wish to explore whether a relationship between two variables is spurious – in other words whether there is another variable which causes the variation in the original two. For example, we might discover a strong relationship between the amount of praise given to pupils in class and their performance in an achievement test, but, on further investigation, find that there is also a relationship between the amount of teaching time pupils receive and their achievements. It seems possible that the relationship between praise and achievement is spurious – changes in both could be caused by the amount of teaching time. Testing for this involves looking at the relationship between praise and achievement at different levels of teaching time. Do we still find a relationship between praise and achievement where pupils receive small and large amounts of teaching time? If we do not then the relationship is probably spurious, but if we do then it is probably non-spurious. In effect what we are doing here is to look at the relationship between two variables whilst controlling statistically for the effect of a third.

This sort of statistical control is often used in educational research which aims to explore the impact of different educational treatments or experiences on pupil achievement (or outcomes of some sort). Here the variable which researchers usually wish to control is pupils' prior achievement or ability. This is done by examining the relationship between treatments and outcomes for pupils at similar prior achievement or ability levels. This basic idea underpins much recent research on school effectiveness (see Rutter *et al.*, 1979; Mortimore *et al.*, 1988; Smith and Tomlinson, 1989).

Another possibility researchers sometimes explore is that a relationship between two variables may be moderated by another variable (or other variables). This means that the relationship holds for some categories of cases but not for others. For instance, in our example of new disciplinary procedures, discussed above, the researcher may find that there is a strong positive relationship between new procedures and pupil behaviour for boys, but not for girls – that the new procedures appear to reduce the amount of disruptive behaviour from boys, but not from girls. Again exploring this possibility involves statistical control. In this case the variable of gender would be controlled.

A third type of multivariate relationship of interest might be multiple causation. Educational phenomena rarely have a single cause and researchers are often interested in identifying the various causal factors and exploring their relative importance. Again they often do this by examining relationships between pairs of variables whilst statistically controlling others. Those variables which reduce the strength of the relationships between others are seen as more important. For example, a researcher might be interested in exploring the relative importance of a number of classroom factors in explaining differences in pupil progress in reading. (Note here that by examining pupils' progress the researcher is controlling in the research design for prior achievement.) He or she might decide to look at variables such as the length of time spent reading to teachers, the regularity of reading in class, or the time at which reading occurred. These decisions would be based upon theoretical ideas the researcher wished to test and would clearly influence the type of data collected. He or she would then explore the relationships between each of these independent variables and the dependent variable whilst controlling for the other two. If, for example, a stronger relationship was discovered between time spent reading and progress when the two other variables are controlled, than was found between time of reading and progress with the two other variables controlled, then this would indicate that time spent reading was the more important variable.

Sometimes relationships between three or more variables are explored using cross-tabulations and tests of statistical significance. They may also involve using partial correlation. Here the correlation between two variables is calculated after controlling for the effect of others. Another technique sometimes used is multiple regression. This involves expressing the relationship between a dependent and a number of independent variables in an equation. This has a series of regression coefficients each expressing the amount of change in the dependent variable which would be produced by changes in each independent variable with the others controlled. This allows the researcher to establish the relative importance of each independent variable to the dependent variable.[8] The result of this sort of analysis is sometimes complex path diagrams indicating relationships between variables and the proportion of the variance on dependent variables which can be predicted by various independent variables. Whilst this sort of complex multivariate analysis can in theory be conducted using observational data, in practice it is rare because resources often do not permit the collection of information on a large number of cases and variables. It is more common in the analysis of survey data because such information can be collected more economically.

A final possibility in the analysis of three or more variables is combining data on different variables together. Sometimes several variables may be strongly related and can therefore be seen as dimensions or aspects of another variable at a higher level of analysis. As Croll (1986) points out, this is essentially the same as factor analysis which is frequently used in attitude measurement. Here variations on a series of attitudinal measures are seen as making up an over-arching variable such as 'liberalism' or 'ethnocentrism'. The same ideas apply in measures of ability, achievement, personality, and so on. Observational variables can sometimes be combined with other variables in the same way to form higher level variables. For example, we might find that data on a number of variables concerning pupils' behaviour – things like attendance at school, truancy, lateness to lessons, incidence of disruptive behaviour, etc. – could be combined to form a composite variable such as 'orientation to school'. In effect the individual behavioural variables here are treated as indicators of different dimensions of the concept of 'orientation to school'.

CONCLUSION

Researchers typically collect large amounts of data on the phenomena they investigate. The basic function of data analysis is to summarize this data and identify the significant features and patterns it reveals about the phenomena of concern. Analysis enables researchers to produce the generalized descriptions, evaluations and explanations which are their main aim.

It has often been suggested that analysis requires radically different procedures depending on whether the data are qualitative or quantitative. Whilst there clearly are differences in technique what I hope this discussion has highlighted is that there are considerable procedural similarities. Of fundamental importance is that the analysis of both types of data is based on comparisons. When analysing qualitative material, pieces of data are compared to develop category systems through which the key features and patterns in the data can be described. With quantitative data, category systems have already been developed, and the search for descriptive features and patterns involves comparisons between the frequency with which instances are allocated to different categories across different units of analysis. In producing evaluations comparisons are made between ideal, or preferred, models and the reality which is observed by the researcher. Finally, when developing explanations researchers compare data categorized in similar and in different ways to search for factors which might indicate relationships between categories.

It is also important to emphasize that these comparisons are not conducted haphazardly. Data analysis is guided along certain tracks by the questions which the researcher sets out to investigate and by theoretical expectations about the nature or causes of the phenomena being studied. This does not, of course, mean that what the researcher finds will merely be a product of these expectations or will simply confirm them. Interesting and unexpected findings can often emerge from data collection and analysis. Indeed, researchers must be constantly aware of and open to these possibilities, and be prepared to submit their expectations to the stringent tests of empirical enquiry.

NOTES

1. Hargreaves says little about the nature of teacher talk which was not about radical innovation, or about talk not categorized as contrastive rhetoric or extremist talk.

2. Quantification in qualitative research is often implicit (in my view a significant weakness) and is characterized by the use of general and ambiguous quantitative terms. We read, for example, that a behaviour occurred 'commonly', 'rarely', 'frequently', or 'occasionally', or that it took up a 'large' or 'small' proportion of a subject's time, or that 'most' or 'few' subjects behaved in a particular way.

3. It is possible to conceive of data from continuous recording as a continuous stream of tallies or codes.

4. Readers planning to conduct these calculations should consult key textbooks on quantitative data analysis and statistics – see for example Bryman and Cramer, 1990, Cramer, 1994.

5. He also tried to explain the patterns of behaviour he observed in the classrooms by reference to the attitudes of the teachers which he measured using a questionnaire.

6. A slightly different approach is analytic induction. On this see Hammersley and Atkinson, 1995.

7. Abraham (1989, 1995) has subsequently added to this work.

8. Where two or more of the independent variables themselves have a strong relationship it is difficult to assess their independent influence.

5

Assessing the Findings of Observational Research

Books on research methodology devote considerable attention to the way research should be conducted, but relatively little to how completed research should be judged by the audiences who read it. A variety of people read research about schools – academic educationalists, policy-makers, practitioners, and sometimes parents. They often read research for different purposes, but, in my view, if they are to make optimum use of research findings, they should not simply accept them without question. Research reports should be viewed critically and assessed for what they can tell us of significance about the topics to which they refer. This chapter discusses the criteria by which research findings should be assessed and explores the process of assessment using two illustrative examples.

THE PROBLEM OF ASSESSMENT CRITERIA

In the last 20 years there has been considerable debate about the criteria against which research in education and the social sciences ought to be assessed (see Smith, 1993 for a review). The traditional positivist or empiricist view, dominant until recently, was that research findings could and should be judged in terms of their validity – whether or not they accurately represent the reality they purport to describe or explain. Good research, from this point of view, establishes the truth about the world, and true accounts directly correspond with the reality they represent. If possible, assessing the validity of research findings requires checking them against reality by replication. Alternatively, or in addition, the researcher's methods must be scrutinized to see whether the research was conducted rigorously and objectively using established scientific procedures, and therefore whether the empirical data on which the findings were based were free from error.

In recent years the epistemological basis of this approach has been severely undermined. It has been pointed out that knowledge claims can never be established with absolute certainty. There will always be doubts about their validity and we can never therefore discover *the* truth about the world. It has also been argued that sense data are inevitably processed by the researcher in the light of his or her existing knowledge, conceptual schemata, theories and values. As a result researchers have no direct access to reality and therefore can never know for certain whether an account corresponds with that reality. Similarly, it has been claimed that since researchers can never completely detach themselves from their existing knowledge and values, it is impossible for them to apply scientific methods objectively.

These criticisms have called into question the criteria and procedures by which research findings have been traditionally assessed. A number of alternative views have been proposed. One of these is relativism. Here the suggestion is that since knowledge claims are inevitably a product of particular cognitive and value frameworks, the validity of claims can only be judged in relation to these frameworks. According to this view, therefore, there are no universal criteria for judging research claims and no standardized procedures for making assessments. Consequently, we must accept that there may be different and possibly competing views about the nature of reality all of which may be judged valid in their own terms. We can have dialogues about these views, but in the end it is not possible to say which is the most valid.

Another approach has developed from critical theory, which has its roots in European Marxism. Here it is suggested that members of oppressed groups – for example the working class, women, or ethnic minorities – or their intellectual representatives (critical theorists) – have privileged access to the truth about the world, and that the role of research is to make clear this reality and to explore the way it is distorted by ideology of a capitalist or technocratic nature. According to this view, research must be judged by the extent to which this is achieved. It should also be judged by its effects – by how successful it is in promoting or inspiring the empowerment or emancipation of oppressed groups. In other words, what is argued is that research should be judged by the criterion of validity, but this is defined as representations which are free of ideological distortion *and* which have emancipatory consequences.

As Hammersley (1995, developed in Foster, Gomm and Hammersley, 1996) has argued, both these approaches are unsatisfactory. Relativism is self-undermining:

> if the validity of all arguments is framework-relative then so is the validity of the claim that the validity of all arguments is framework-relative. And this implies that even from the relativist point of view, while true for relativists, relativism is false for non-relativists.
>
> (Foster, Gomm and Hammersley, 1996, p. 37).

Moreover, in suggesting that it is not possible to choose between divergent knowledge claims relativism seems to undercut the very possibility of knowledge itself.

The views derived from critical theory are also highly questionable. Whilst we must recognize that people's social position gives them a distinctive perspective on reality, it is not clear why we should accept the view that some positions give groups greater access to reality than others. Such arguments themselves seem little more than ideological. Furthermore, as Foster, Gomm and Hammersley (1996) point out, treating desirable consequences as indicators of validity 'assumes a much stronger relationship between the truth of a belief and the practical consequences of acting on it than is justifiable: the validity of assumptions is neither a necessary nor a sufficient condition of practical success'(p. 37).

Hammersley argues that both these approaches are over-reactions to the epistemological problems of positivist empiricism. He suggests that it is possible to resolve these problems by adopting a position of 'subtle realism', rather than the 'naive realism' which characterized positivism (see Hammersley, 1990a, 1992, 1995). This position recognizes that it is impossible to produce knowledge of reality which is absolutely certain, but maintains that we can strive for knowledge about which we can be reasonably confident. In other words it acknowledges that we can never discover *the* truth about the world, but argues that we can move towards a position where there is a high probability of truth.

What this means for the assessment of research claims is that we can, and should, maintain a commitment to validity as a universal criterion, but define this in terms of the likelihood that research claims correspond to reality. In Hammersley's view such assessments can be conducted by examining the plausibility and credibility of research claims. By 'plausible' he means judging whether a claim is 'very likely to be true given our existing knowledge' (Hammersley, 1990a, p. 61). If our judgement is that the claim is highly plausible, then we can usually accept it at face value. If not, then we need to examine its credibility – whether it is likely to be true 'given the nature of the phenomena concerned, the circumstances of the research, the characteristics of the researcher, etc.'(p. 61). Judging credibility involves considering the possibility of errors occurring in the collection, analysis and interpretation of evidence, and examining any checks on validity which have been performed. If, after considering these matters, our judgement is that the claim is credible, then we would accept it. If not, then we would require evidence before we could accept it, and we would assess the plausibility and credibility of this evidence in the same way.

Hammersley notes that this process of assessment is somewhat different depending on the type of claim being made. Simplifying his discussion somewhat, he distinguishes between three main types of claim – descriptions and explanations, which are factual claims, and evaluations. Descriptions are representations of the features of some phenomenon, explanations are claims about why some phenomenon has the features it does, and evaluations are claims about the desirability of the particular features of a phenomenon. Assessing descriptive claims usually involves examining evidence from two sources – the researcher's observations and/or informants' accounts (and, of course, it is the former type of evidence we are concerned with in this book). Judging explanatory claims requires an assessment of their descriptive components (since all explanations are based on descriptions), but in addition the reader must assess the theoretical plausibility of the explanation, the chronology of cause and effect suggested, and possibility of alternative explanations (see Chapter 4). Judging an evaluation also requires an assessment of component descriptions, but must also consider whether the value judgement is justified on the basis of the ideal or preferred model employed, and given other values which could, or should, have been taken into account.

Different readers may, of course, make different judgements about the validity of claims using these procedures. This is particularly likely where value judgements are involved, but it is also possible because researchers differ about the amount or strength of evidence required to establish factual claims. As a result there may be significant disagreements about the current state of knowledge on a particular issue. Hammersley (1992) suggests the solution to this problem is to utilize the practice, long institutionalized to one degree or another in universities, of rational discussion directed towards reaching agreement and establishing common ground. He argues that researchers should

> seek to establish their findings as sufficiently plausible and credible to be accepted not only from their own point of view, but also by anticipating the likely judgements of fellow researchers. In writing their research reports they should provide sufficient evidence to convince that audience; and, in the face of expressions of doubt, they should be prepared to supply further evidence.
>
> (Hammersley, 1992, p. 70)

Thus, Hammersley suggests where readers express reasonable doubts about the validity of research claims, the onus should be on the researcher to provide further evidence or supporting argument. If this is unforthcoming then judgement should be suspended for want of the necessary evidence or support. This does not, of course, mean those claims are therefore false, merely that sufficient evidence or support has not been presented to enable us to accept them as likely to be true.

Hammersley (1990a) also argues that research claims should be assessed against the criterion of relevance. By this he means that the research should provide information related to an issue of public concern. He points out that there is little purpose in conducting research which is irrelevant to any such concern, although we should beware of narrow conceptions of these matters. He suggests that there are two aspects of relevance:

1) The importance of the topic. The research topic must relate (however remotely) to an issue of public importance.

2) The contribution of the conclusions to existing knowledge. The research findings must add something to our knowledge of the issue to which they relate. Research that merely confirms what is already beyond reasonable doubt makes no contribution.

> (Hammersley, 1990a, p. 107)

Hammersley's proposals provide a solution to the problem of criteria which recognizes the untenability of positivist empiricism, but avoids the pitfalls of relativism and the politically orientated assumptions of critical theory. They provide a way of assessing research findings – both qualitative and quantitative – in terms of their probable truth, by examining their plausibility and credibility. For most research studies it is the latter criterion which is most important as findings of any significance are unlikely to be sufficiently plausible to be accepted at face value. Thus, before looking at how we can apply his proposals to particular research studies, we need to examine the notion of credibility in a little more depth focusing on its application to descriptive claims, since these provide the basis of all research claims.

THREATS TO VALIDITY IN OBSERVATIONAL RESEARCH

Hammersley suggests that in assessing the credibility of descriptive claims based on observational data we need to be aware of the various possibilities of error in the production of these claims. I will discuss these briefly in relation to the stages of observational research we discussed in Chapters 2, 3 and 4.[1]

One possibility is that errors arise from decisions made about what to observe. Sometimes important aspects of the phenomena of concern are not observed resulting in a partial and incomplete view. This may happen because the focus of the research was not clearly defined, because the data relevant to the focus was not clearly specified, or because ideas about focus and relevance changed during the course of data collection. This problem is most likely to occur in less structured research where a clear focus may not emerge until well into the fieldwork. It may also occur when access to important situations is denied or restricted by gatekeepers or by a lack of resources.

Errors can also occur where the selection of observational cases or instances is unrepresentative of the population to which the claims refer, or, if theoretical sampling is involved, where the cases or instances selected do not allow an adequate test of the theory under consideration. The result may be invalid inference about the population or theory on the basis of what is observed. As readers what we need here is evidence to allow us to judge whether the observed sample is representative in relevant respects of the heterogeneity in the target population, or alternatively whether the characteristics of the cases or instances are such that they can provide a reasonable test of the theory.

Another possibility is that error occurs as a result of the subjects' perception of the research procedures or the researcher. Sometimes subjects change their behaviour because they are aware of being observed or because the research disrupts their normal environment. This might happen, for example, in experimental research where subjects are placed in artificial situations and what goes on is deliberately manipulated, or where video recording necessitates adjustments to the classroom environment. This is often referred to as procedural reactivity.

Subjects may also behave differently in response to the characteristics or behaviour of the observer – what is termed personal reactivity. For instance, they may react in particular ways because the observer is male or female or from a certain ethnic group, or because he or she dresses or conducts him or herself in a particular way. Moreover, where two or more observers are involved, as is sometimes the case in larger projects, subjects may react differently with different observers, creating problems of reliability too.

A third possible area of errors is in the recording of observations. The observer may misinterpret what he or she sees, hears, etc. and therefore make an inaccurate record of the actual behaviour. This is more likely where the behaviour under study is complex or when the observer is unfamiliar with the social situation and the meanings in play.

Recording errors are also more likely when certain recording techniques are used. Most problematic here is when observations are noted down sometime after they are made – for example, when field notes are written in the evening, the following day or even later. In such situations memory lapses can result in significant loss of data and distortion.

Errors can also result from inadequacies in the recording systems employed in more structured observation. The preconceived categories of the observation system may be unsuitable for recording the actual nature of the behaviour observed. They may ignore aspects of behaviour which are important given the aims of the research or they may force the observer to code under the same category behaviour which is significantly different. Moreover, there may be ambiguities in category definitions and in the procedures for allocating instances to categories which result in unreliability, particularly where a number of researchers are involved.

Errors can also occur at the analysis stage. Even when all relevant data has been collected it may not be retrieved (or a representative sample may not be retrieved) from the data store for analysis. This is a problem particularly in qualitative research where large amounts of data are collected and stored under diverse and flexible headings. Recent developments in computer storage and search and retrieval facilities have helped somewhat here, although their effectiveness is dependent on the original data coding.

Conceptual and coding ambiguity can also result in error in the analysis of qualitative data. As in more structured observation, where coding occurs at the point of observation, the definitions of conceptual categories and the rules for assigning instances to categories may be unclear, so that there may be confusion during the analysis about how the categories are applied. Where quantification is involved there may also be a lack of clarity in the calculation of the frequency or intensity of categories. In the absence of clear measurement systems it is possible that qualitative researchers are unduly influenced by instances that fit their expectations or which are unusual or novel, or by patterns which occur early in the fieldwork (Sadler, 1982).

Errors can also occur in the analysis of quantitative data. Inappropriate statistical techniques may be used and mistakes can be made in calculations, especially where these are conducted by hand. Moreover, inappropriate inferences may be made on the basis of statistically summarized data. For example, it might be concluded that two sets of scores are similar because they have similar means, whereas in fact the range of scores in the two sets are very different, or a correlation may be seen as indicating a causal relationship between two variables, whereas in reality the relationship is spurious.

In assessing the credibility of the findings of observational research we must be aware that these types of error can occur. In our reading of research we must judge how likely it was that they occurred and how significant they were for the validity of the findings. A number of factors influence the likelihood of significant error – the complexity of the topic being studied, constraints operating in the research setting, the adequacy of the resources available, the expertise of the researcher, and so on – and information on these is relevant to any judgement. Perhaps one factor worth singling out is the possibility of researcher bias. The researcher's preconceived theories, values, or political commitments may result in significant error in a particular direction. Bias may, of course, be difficult to detect. However, certain information may alert readers to the possibility. For example, details of the researcher's commitments and information on the political orientation of sponsoring organizations would be useful – though we should not assume bias if there are strong commitments in either case. Perhaps most important is an examination of the research itself to check if there is a tendency for errors or interpretations of evidence to be slanted consistently in a particular direction.

Also useful to any judgement of the probability of error is information about any checks on validity and reliability which the researcher has performed. In more structured observation researchers sometimes examine the extent of agreement between two observers of the same behaviour. Sometimes individual coding decisions of two observers are compared; this is termed absolute agreement. Alternatively, the overall coding results are compared to see whether the total number of behaviours allocated to the categories of the system tally; this is called marginal agreement. Clearly, absolute agreement is a much stronger check of the reliability of the observations, but it is not always possible to conduct such a test with all observation systems. Inter-observer agreement is usually worked out for each category of the observation system and is expressed as the proportion of individual or total codings which are the same.

In less structured observation, techniques such as reflexivity, triangulation and respondent validation are more often used. Reflexivity involves the researcher monitoring, and reflecting on, his or her own influence, and on the effect of social context, on data production. He or she constantly scrutinizes the production of data, considering potential sources of error, and evaluating his or her own role. Where we know such an approach has been consciously adopted we can be more confident that data and research findings are free from error.

Triangulation involves checking the validity of findings and/or observational data themselves by cross-checking with other sources of data. If research findings or data are supported by data from other sources then we can be more confident about their validity. In triangulating researchers can compare observational data on the same behaviour from different researchers (as in the reliability checks of more structured observation) who possibly adopt different roles in the field. Alternatively, they can compare data produced by different methods – for example, observational data can be compared with interview data or data from key informants.

Respondent validation involves checking the validity of the researcher's observations by reference to the subjects' perceptions. The researcher may discuss his or her observations with subjects asking them whether they are accurate and what their perceptions of particular incidents were, or he or she may ask subjects for written accounts of particular events which can then be compared with his or her own.

Of course, respondent validation or the use of informants' accounts in triangulation does not automatically ensure the accuracy of data or findings. Subjects or informants may be concerned to manipulate the impression of behaviour which is contained in the data as a way of enhancing or protecting their own interests and they may therefore present or interpret behaviour in particular ways. Their accounts will be influenced by the social context in which they are delivered, and by their perceptions of the researcher and of the use to which the data will be put. Moreover, it is important to recognize that subjects' and informants' accounts are usually reconstructions from memory which may be subject to error. In fact, we must recognize and assess the potential threats to validity in these accounts in the same way as we assess those in researchers' observations. Nevertheless, information about triangulation and respondent validation provide readers with more evidence on which they can assess the likely validity of research findings.

TWO EXAMPLES

To illustrate the process of assessing the findings of observational research let me consider two studies on a similar topic which use different observational approaches.[2] The first is a study of teacher–pupil relationships and interactions in four multi-ethnic primary schools conducted by Cecile Wright (1992) which used less structured, ethnographic methods. The second is an examination of teacher–pupil interaction in the multi-ethnic classrooms of 70 middle and junior school teachers conducted by Peter Green (1983) which employed a more structured approach. Both studies were essentially concerned with whether ethnic minority students are treated equitably in comparison to ethnic majority students in schools. Their claims are therefore evaluative as well as descriptive, though in both studies the evaluative standards are implicit. Green's study also contains explanatory elements as he relates the patterns of classroom interaction he observed to teachers' attitudes and to students' self-esteem.

Wright spent about a term in each of the schools she studied observing school life, talking to teachers, pupils and parents, and examining documents of various sorts (I will focus here on the aspects of Wright's study which are based on observational data). She claims that on the surface the schools were characterized by a pleasant and caring atmosphere which took account of the needs of different groups of children, but that her observations 'revealed subtle differences in the way white teachers treated black children' (p. 15).[3] She claims that Asian children 'received the least attention from the teacher' (p. 17), and were rarely invited to join in classroom discussion. She also reports that teachers frequently responded negatively to them when their language difficulties or cultural differences created problems for classroom management or teaching effectiveness, and that they were regularly rejected and harassed by their white peers. Similarly, Wright argues that teachers had negative expectations of Afro-Caribbean children, who were 'always amongst the most criticized and controlled group in the classroom' (p. 57). These children, she claims, were often 'singled out for reprimanding even where several children of different groups were engaged in the same act or behaviour' (p. 101). Wright also maintains that the teachers' efforts to encourage multiculturalism in the classroom often backfired, because of their lack of confidence and understanding, and resulted in the embarrassment of black children. Lying behind these descriptive claims are implicit evaluative claims. Wright is clearly arguing that this differential treatment is inequitable and therefore undesirable.

In my view, our limited knowledge of these issues combined with their complexity means that none of Wright's claims is sufficiently plausible or credible to be accepted at face value. Evidence is therefore required to convince me of their validity, and in several places in her report Wright provides quite detailed evidence. This consists mainly of descriptive accounts of her observations of selected classroom incidents derived from field notes and tape transcripts. This is sometimes supplemented by informants' accounts, mainly from Afro-Caribbean nursery nurses and carers, and a small number of Afro-Caribbean and Asian children. Wright also utilizes a number of general comments from the teachers derived from interviews and classroom logs.

There are, however, some problems with the evidence Wright presents which raise significant doubts about the validity of her claims. First, some of her claims are not actually supported by the evidence she presents – for instance, her claim that Asian children were given less teacher attention than other groups and that they were rarely encouraged to take part in classroom discussion. These claims concern quantitative differences between groups in terms of overall teacher attention and particular types of attention. They therefore require some quantitative data derived from clear measurement of the distribution of attention to children of different ethnic groups to support them. Wright does not provide this, relying instead on her own informal impressions.

A related problem is that her observational accounts refer to single incidents whereas her claims are about regularities and common patterns of behaviour. Teachers, Wright maintains, *often* responded negatively to Asian children and *more often* criticized Afro-Caribbean children and singled them out for reprimand. But she gives no quantitative data on the frequency of these occurrences, nor does she explain how instances of 'negative response', 'criticism' or 'singling children out for reprimand', were defined and counted. She also does not explain how the treatment of Asian and Afro-Caribbean children in these respects was compared to the treatment of white children. Her judgement here appears to be impressionistic and therefore highly likely to be subject to the sorts of error we discussed earlier.

Another problem is that these incidents are presented as typical of the way the individual teachers, and the teachers in the four schools, routinely treated ethnic minority children, or as typical of the experiences of individual ethnic minority children, and ethnic minority children in general, in the four schools. Yet Wright presents no evidence to support these generalizations. It is difficult to accept their validity on the basis of single incidents, without further information to support their representativeness.

A further problem with Wright's evidence is that many of her interpretations of the classroom incidents she describes are questionable. One example is her report of an incident (pp. 16–17) in which a teacher has problems conveying instructions and the meaning of a word to an Asian girl, and so asks another Asian girl to translate. The second girl does not speak or help, a response which seems to irritate the teacher. Wright interprets this as an instance of the teacher's expression of annoyance at 'the Asian children's poor English language skills'. However, it might just as easily be seen as the teacher responding to the second girl's apparent refusal to co-operate. Indeed, the teacher says to the child 'you're supposed to be helping' (p. 17).

Another example is Wright's description of a teacher–group discussion in a nursery class which she claims shows an Afro-Caribbean boy (Marcus) being reprimanded by the teacher for shouting out when others in the group were also shouting out (pp. 19–21). Wright interprets this as an instance of the teacher responding more harshly to Afro-Caribbean children behaving in the same way as white children, as a result of her negative expectations. However, it is difficult to tell from Wright's description whether Marcus' behaviour actually was the same as others who were not reprimanded. His shouting out may have been more extreme or accompanied by other disruptive behaviour.

Indeed, there is a complex issue here about what 'the same behaviour' means. Does it mean the same from an observer's point of view or from the teacher's point of view? From an observer's point of view students' behaviour may be interpreted as the same. But from the teacher's point of view it may not, because it is seen in the context of what is happening more generally in the classroom at that time, what has happened in the recent past, and what typifications and expectations the teacher has of the students involved. The observer has no immediate access to much of this contextual information, and Wright does not explore it by seeking the teacher's perspective on the incident.

She relies on her own observer's perspective thus interpreting behaviour to some extent 'out of context' from the teacher's point of view. Wright does not consider these conceptual complexities and does not therefore adequately establish the similarity of the behaviour to which the teacher was responding. Nor does she establish that Marcus' differential treatment was caused by the teacher's expectations of bad behaviour from Afro-Caribbean children. It may have been, but equally it may have been the product of her expectation of bad behaviour from Marcus himself, an expectation which may or may not have been well founded.

Wright's interpretations of some of the teachers' comments in interviews and classroom logs is similarly problematic. She tends to interpret negative comments about individual Afro-Caribbean children as indicating teachers' negative views about Afro-Caribbean children in general. She infers from this that the teachers responded to Afro-Caribbean children in terms of negative racial stereotypes. This may have been the case, but Wright's data does not establish it.

It is important to note here that Wright's interpretations of her data are consistently in the same direction, i.e. towards a claim of racial or ethnic discrimination on the part of teachers. None of the data she presents is interpreted in ways which are more favourable to the teachers, even though such interpretations are clearly possible. This alerts me to the possibility of bias in her account. This suspicion is reinforced by the other inadequacies in her evidence, by the lack of respondent validation on the particular incidents Wright describes, and by the absence of any evidence of reflection by Wright on the role of her own values in the construction of her account.

The problems I have outlined lead me to conclude that there is a high probability of significant error in the production of Wright's descriptive claims about the four schools. I cannot therefore accept their validity. This does not, of course, mean that they are necessarily untrue, merely that adequate evidence has not been provided to convince me that they are true.

Wright's failure to establish her descriptive claims also, of course, means that the evaluative aspects of her work cannot be accepted either. Here, however, there are further problems. Wright is not at all clear about the model of good practice that lies behind her work. In fact she appears to operate on the basis of several models. For example, in places she seems to base her claims on the view that children from different ethnic groups should receive equal amounts of teacher attention or teacher attention of particular types. In other places she seems to ground her arguments on the idea that teachers should respond to the same behaviour from students in the same way. We might question the desirability of both these models. As regards the first, while we might accept that all students should have some teacher attention, it could be argued that it is the quality of attention students receive which is important, rather than the amount. Moreover, there are sometimes strong cases for giving some students more, and others less, teacher attention. Regarding the second, as I have already indicated, the notion of 'same behaviour' can be interpreted differently and this will influence judgements about the desirability of this value. Moreover, powerful arguments can be made in favour of the view that teachers should adjust their responses to the characteristics of the individual child, and therefore not respond to the 'same behaviour' from different children in the same way. Indeed, such arguments are frequently put forward by advocates of anti-racism. We might also question the compatibility of these two models. Responding to the same behaviour from children in the same way may result in giving some children more total attention or more attention of certain types simply because they behave more often in particular ways. In short, Wright has not clarified sufficiently the values or the notion of good practice on which her evaluative claims are based.

Green's claims are similar to Wright's in that he argues that ethnic minority students received a differential allocation of certain types of teacher attention in comparison to ethnic majority students in the classrooms of the teachers he observed. Green used Flanders' Interaction Analysis System (see Chapter 1) to record the interaction of teachers with 'West Indian', 'Asian' and 'European' students. He reports that there were significant differences in interaction patterns in the classrooms of teachers who, on the basis of questionnaire responses, were classified as ethnically 'highly tolerant' or 'highly intolerant'.[4] He suggests that in the classrooms of the 12 highly intolerant teachers West Indian students received less of the teaching categories 'accepts feeling', 'praise or encouragement', 'acceptance/use of pupils' ideas', 'direct teaching', but more 'criticism or justification of authority', than their European and Asian peers. Also, West Indian students were less likely to initiate contributions and respond to their teachers. In contrast, in the classrooms of the 12 highly tolerant teachers European students received less of the categories 'accepts feeling' (boys only), 'praise or encouragement', 'acceptance/use of pupils' ideas', 'asks questions, and giving directions' than their Asian or West Indian peers; and they were also less likely to initiate contributions and respond to their teachers. Green explains these differences in interaction patterns by reference to the differences in the teachers' attitudes to ethnicity. He also implies that the patterns of interaction he observed, particularly in the classrooms of ethnically intolerant teachers, were inequitable.

Again these claims are neither sufficiently plausible nor credible to be accepted at face value. They require evidence in their support. In producing this evidence Green, unlike Wright, did try to measure systematically differences in the teachers' interaction with students from different ethnic groups. However, his evidence too suffers from a number of major weaknesses.

The first relates to his use of the Flanders schedule. This is not usually used to measure how much of the different interactional categories are devoted to particular groups, and so Green had to modify the coding to record the particular ethnic group to which each type of interaction was directed. But this seems to introduce difficult problems with several of the categories of teacher behaviour in the Flanders system. It is often very difficult for an observer to tell which student, or category of student, a teacher's behaviour is directed towards, particularly when the observer is coding behaviour at 3 second intervals, which is the recognized practice with this system.

Another problem is that it is often difficult reliably to allocate behaviour to the categories of the Flanders schedule. The categories themselves and the coding rules are rather ambiguous, so that there may have been errors in Green's allocation of observed events to categories. Green says little about the problem of reliability except to indicate that he was experienced in using the schedule and all coding was carried out by one observer. This is reassuring in some respects, but it does not ensure high reliability. There may have been inconsistency in Green's coding such that if the same classrooms had been observed by another researcher there might have been different results.

A final problem with Green's use of the Flanders system is that it is designed to code public teacher–student interaction which is easily observable. It is not very suitable for use in classrooms where teachers interact more privately with students in small groups or individually, and these types of interaction are very common in most junior and middle schools. In these situations it is difficult to code interaction accurately because it may take place beyond the observer's hearing or view. These problems all give rise to significant doubts about the validity of Green's observational data.

A second major weakness is that Green does not present data on individual teachers. He groups his data on the 12 highly tolerant and 12 highly intolerant teachers calculating the total amount of each type of interaction received by students of different ethnic groups in the classes of all 12 teachers. As readers, we do not therefore know whether the patterns he identified were characteristic of each teacher's lesson, or were produced by a small number of teachers who interacted with their students in particularly extreme ways.

This point relates to the problem of the generalizations Green makes on the basis of his data. Whilst Green studied a relatively large number of teachers which provided a stronger basis for generalization to the wider population of teachers, the resources available to him meant he could only observe each teacher for one lesson. Green assumed that the patterns of interaction he observed in these single lessons were typical of the patterns which occurred more generally in these teachers' lessons. Unfortunately, he gives no evidence to support this generalization, and there must therefore be doubts about the representativeness of the lessons he observed.

As with Wright's research, these problems raise significant doubts about the validity of Green's descriptive claims. The chances of error in the production of his claims appears to be quite high, and again I am not therefore inclined to accept them on the basis of the evidence he presents. Moreover, similar problems arise to those with Wright's research about the nature and desirability of the evaluative standards which underpin his work.

Green's failure to establish his descriptive claims also, of course, undermines his explanatory claim – that the differential treatment he observed was caused by differences in the teachers' attitudes. But, even if his descriptive claims were well established, there would be further problems here. We might question the validity of his measurement of teachers' attitudes but, setting this aside, there seem to be other possible explanations for the patterns of interaction which Green does not consider. For example, it may be that they were caused by differences in the students' behaviour to which the teachers were responding. The Flanders system did not allow Green to record data on this variable, and this is clearly a threat to the validity of his explanation.

My assessment of these two studies has been conducted so far on the basis of Hammersley's first criterion – validity. In both cases I have argued there are serious doubts about the validity of the claims advanced by these two researchers. How do they stand up against his second criterion – relevance? In my view both studies address an issue of public importance. The question of whether ethnic minority students are treated equitably in education is a subject of considerable concern and relates to a key value principle in our society – equal opportunity. There is a lot of debate about how such principles can be realized, and the extent to which they are in fact realized, in education and beyond. Research which provides accurate information about these matters is a valuable resource in these debates. It should, in theory, place decisions about policy and practice on a much sounder footing.

But the problem with both the studies I have discussed is that, because there are serious doubts about the validity of their findings, they make only a very limited contribution to existing knowledge on the topic to which they relate. Here we can see the link between the criteria of validity and relevance. If we conclude that research findings are not valid – in other words we do not judge them to be likely to be true on the basis of the evidence presented – then they cannot advance our knowledge on the particular issue of concern. Thus even if they address an issue of importance we must judge them of limited relevance. This, then, is my view about the two studies we have considered here.[5]

In making this judgement I do not wish to suggest that these studies are worthless. There is perhaps another way in which they add significantly to our knowledge. In attempting to explore a complex topic using particular methods they have alerted us to the advantages, and more importantly the limitations, of these methods. They have therefore advanced our methodological knowledge, and enabled us, as researchers, to decide better what methods and resources are required to advance knowledge in this area in the future.

CONCLUSION

In this chapter I have discussed the criteria by which the findings of observational research can be assessed, and have argued in favour of the adoption of Hammersley's (1990a) suggested criteria of validity and relevance. It is important to emphasize that in advocating the criterion of validity Hammersley is not suggesting that we can ever be absolutely certain that accounts of the world correspond to reality, since we have no direct access to that reality. He argues that we must accept uncertainty, and all we can therefore do is assess the likely truth of research findings. This, he suggests, we should do by judging the plausibility and credibility of research findings and the evidence on which they are based.

I then illustrated the way these criteria could be applied to two research studies based on different observational approaches to the topic of racial or ethnic equality. In my view both these studies suffer from severe methodological problems which raise serious doubts about the validity of their findings. But these problems are not uncommon ones in educational research; they are not restricted to these studies.

Of course, all observational research on schools does not suffer from the same problems. In some studies there are problems deriving from some of the other threats to validity we have discussed. In other studies threats to validity are not as severe as in the two studies I have assessed. In the latter case we can be much more confident about the likely truth of claims and therefore about the contribution which is made to knowledge in a particular area.

My main point in this chapter is that research findings should not be accepted unquestioningly. They should be scrutinized and assessed for what they can tell us about the topic they have investigated. This scrutiny requires careful attention to the claims themselves, the way they are produced, and the evidence on which they are based.

NOTES

1.   For a more detailed, and different order of, discussion see Foster, Gomm and Hammersley, 1996.

2.   For further examples of evaluations of research studies see Foster, 1990b, 1993a; Hammersley 1990a, 1990b, 1993; Foster, Gomm and Hammersley, 1996.

3.   She uses the term 'black' to refer to children of Afro-Caribbean and Asian backgrounds.

4.   Green makes many complex claims and I discuss only some aspects of his study here.

5.   This view is not shared by some of the other researchers working in this field. They have more favourable views of these studies and others in the area. They have argued that the evidential requirements that my colleagues and I have applied are too stringent, and that we have adopted a position of 'methodological purism' in assessing research in this area. This debate (see Foster, 1993b; Gillborn and Drew, 1993; Hammersley and Gomm, 1993; Gillborn, 1995; Hammersley, 1995; Troyna, 1995) illustrates how disagreements can occur in a research community about the validity and relevance of studies, and consequently about the current state of knowledge in a particular area.

6

Ethical Issues in Observational Research

Another way in which research can be assessed is in terms of its ethics – the morality of the research itself and of the procedures used – and in recent years there has been considerable criticism of some studies across a range of fields of social inquiry on these grounds. For example, it has been claimed that certain studies have investigated topics of a personal or private nature which should not have been exposed to public scrutiny, that the procedures or outcomes of others have had damaging effects on those involved, and that in some studies researchers have acted dishonestly by deceiving subjects about their real identity, purposes or methods. It has also been argued that some researchers have made exaggerated claims which go beyond the limits of their data, that some have allowed their preconceived views and political commitments to bias their enquiries, and that others have deliberately misrepresented the phenomena they study. Critics maintain that such activities not only contravene important values such as honesty in relationships with research subjects, the pursuit of truth and respect for people's privacy, but they damage the status and future of research itself.

It is not just researchers who have been subject to criticism. Those who sponsor and fund research have been attacked by researchers themselves for exceeding the boundaries of their legitimate influence over research. It has been argued that researchers' academic freedom has been eroded by increasing restrictions on the topics they study and the methods they use, and by attempts to censor and manipulate research findings to suit particular political viewpoints.

A product of these criticisms of, and by, researchers has been the suggestion that key values or ethical principles should guide the planning, conduct and reporting of research. These values have underpinned the development, by a number of subject associations, in recent years of statements, codes or guidelines regarding ethical practice (see, for example, British Sociological Association (BSA), 1992; British Educational Research Association (BERA), 1992; British Psychological Society (BPS), 1995). My aim in this chapter is to consider these values and explore their application to observational research in schools.[1]

THE PURSUIT OF TRUTH

The key value underpinning research is the pursuit of truth. Indeed, most researchers see the production of knowledge about the world as their key goal. They feel that knowledge about the world is preferable to ignorance, and that true information is better than false information, because these allow people to act more appropriately and effectively in the world.

Given this, it is surprising how little attention is devoted to this value in the various ethical statements. That researchers should be committed to the pursuit of truth tends to be stated rather briefly and obliquely. The BSA (1992) statement, for instance, under the heading of 'professional integrity', points to the responsibility of researchers to 'report their findings accurately and truthfully' (p. 1), and, under the heading of 'relations with and responsibilities towards sponsors', states that such relations should 'enable social inquiry to be undertaken as objectively as possible' (p. 2). Similarly, the BERA (1992) guidelines, in the section on 'responsibility to the research profession', state that 'Educational researchers should aim to avoid fabrication, falsification, or misrepresentation of evidence, data, findings, or conclusions' (p. 1); and in a later section on publication explain that a researcher's rights might legitimately be restricted where there is a 'failure to report findings in a manner consistent with the values of inquiry i.e. to report findings honestly, accurately, comprehensively, in context, and without due sensationalisation'(p. 4).

Unfortunately, there is relatively little elaboration in these statements about what a commitment to pursue the truth might mean for research practice. Let me attempt this here. First, I think such a commitment clearly means that researchers should not ('*not*' rather than 'avoid' as the BERA guidelines state) fabricate, falsify or deliberately misrepresent data or findings. This should perhaps go without saying, though there have been cases where it has occurred. The late Cyril Burt, for example, appears to have fabricated some of his data which showed the similarity in intelligence of identical twins (see Diener and Crandall, 1978).

Second, in my view a commitment to truth suggests that researchers should design their studies, and utilize methods of data collection and analysis, in ways which will minimize the sorts of error in the production of evidence and findings we discussed in the last chapter. It also suggests that, within the constraints of the resources available to them, they should also make efforts to check the validity of their data and findings using techniques such as triangulation and respondent validation. Adopting appropriate methods can never, of course, ensure that the truth about a phenomena will be discovered with absolute certainty, but it should maximize the probability that this will occur.

I think a third implication of the pursuit of truth is that researchers should strive for objectivity in conducting their enquiries and not allow their pre-existing theories, knowledge, values or political commitments to bias their collection, interpretation and presentation of evidence and findings. This view, as I noted in the last chapter, has been challenged in recent years by the argument that researchers can never set aside their existing knowledge and values and see the world in a completely detached and objective way. It has been pointed out that the questions researchers address, and what they choose to observe and record, are inevitably the product of their pre-existing theories and often their political commitments, and that their interpretations will always be influenced by their existing conceptual schemata and ways of looking at the world.

I think we must accept some of this argument. Research questions and decisions about what data to collect must, and should, be guided by researchers' pre-existing ideas and concerns. Indeed, without these research would have no focus. It is also inevitable that researchers' existing knowledge and ways of thinking will have some influence on the way data is interpreted. We all make sense of what we see of the world using our existing cultural resources. Thus we must recognize that there is no such thing as total objectivity, in the sense of researchers operating completely independently of these resources.

However, it does not follow from this that the principle of objectivity should be abandoned altogether. There are clear differences between basing research questions on existing theories and commitments and allowing these to determine the results of the enquiry or conducting the research in order to simply confirm them. Similarly, there are differences between interpreting data in the light of existing cultural resources and being confined to single interpretations and blind to the possibility of new or alternative interpretations. In short, there is a difference between the inevitable and legitimate influence of preconceptions, on the one hand, and bias on the other.

In my view it is the latter which researchers should strive to avoid. They can maximize their chances of doing this by adopting three main strategies. They can be open-minded in their approaches. This involves a willingness to consider alternative theoretical and value positions in the framing of their enquiries, to utilize and take account of evidence from a variety of relevant sources, and to actively explore alternative interpretations of evidence, and alternative representations of, and explanations for, the phenomena they are studying.

Researchers can also ground their findings firmly in the data they collect. They can base their conceptual frameworks, models, and theories on careful, thorough and systematic analyses of as much relevant data as possible. They must be aware here of the limitations of their data and take care not to make claims which go beyond what their data can legitimately support. This is sometimes a temptation when researchers' reputations or careers are at stake, or when theoretical and political commitments are strongly held. An important technique in this grounding strategy is to actively explore the field, or the data already collected, for disconfirming evidence. Researchers can search systematically for evidence which might raise doubts about their pre-existing or emerging theories, rather than looking simply for evidence which might support them. Those which survive such tests are more likely to be valid.

Another strategy which researchers can adopt is reflexivity. This involves assessing the influence of their own knowledge, ideas and values on what they choose to study and how they conduct their research, as well as judging their impact as researchers or participants on the phenomenon of concern. In other words, researchers can make active efforts to expose to themselves, and to others, their role in constructing the accounts they present.

A final implication of the commitment to the pursuit of truth is the idea that researchers should open their work to academic scrutiny. I think researchers must be prepared to make information about the way their research was conducted, as well as their findings and the evidence on which they are based, available to others. This will allow readers to evaluate the validity and relevance of their work in the way I outlined in the last chapter. This type of collective scrutiny will increase the chances that errors will be uncovered where they occur and maximize the probability that the truth about the particular phenomena of concern will be discovered. It follows from this that the evaluation of research is an important part of the process of collective enquiry and should therefore play a more important role than it does at present.

These suggestions apply as much to those conducting observational research in schools as they do to social researchers generally. Whether the purpose is the production of knowledge in the traditional academic sense or the development of practice via action research or evaluation, the argument is that the discovery of the truth about the phenomena of interest is of paramount importance. In my view the chances of the truth being discovered will be enhanced by the adoption of the suggestions I have outlined.

However, some provisos are necessary here. Whilst researchers generally see knowledge and the truth as desirable, there are arguments that they should not be pursued at all costs. In some circumstances the production, and more particularly the dissemination, of knowledge can have negative consequences. It can harm individuals, groups or institutions to which the knowledge refers, and may sometimes result in actions which can be seen as undesirable. There are perhaps some phenomena which are best not investigated and some stories best left untold. There is also the argument that the ends sometimes do not justify the means: that truth should not be pursued if doing so overrides other important values such as honesty in relationships with research subjects, respect for subjects' privacy and respect for people's rights to decide whether to be involved in research. Before discussing these values in more depth we need to explore a second principle which is closely associated with the pursuit of truth – academic freedom.

ACADEMIC FREEDOM

The idea of academic freedom suggests that researchers should be able to conduct their research and publish their findings free from undue constraints by government, research funders, colleagues, research participants and others.

The BERA (1992) guidelines give this an especially high priority. Indeed, the main driving force behind the development of this set of guidelines appears to have been the tendency for central government to increase restrictions on the conduct and reporting of the research it funds (see Simons, 1995). The guidelines state that

> Educational researchers should not agree to conduct research that conflicts with academic freedom, nor should they agree to undue or questionable influence by government or other funding agencies. Examples of such improper influence include endeavours to interfere with the conduct of research, the analysis of findings, or the reporting of interpretations.
>
> (BERA, 1992, p. 3)

They also maintain that researchers 'should remain free to interpret and publish their findings without censorship or approval from individuals or organisations, including sponsors, funding agencies, participants, colleagues, supervisors, or administrators' (p. 2).

Academic freedom, it is suggested, allows researchers to pursue important truths about the world unhindered by those who might wish to restrict them to certain issues or constrain them to particular findings. According to this view, researchers' independence allows them to investigate questions that those with vested interests (sometimes, but not always, those in dominant political positions in society or institutions) might not want explored, and enables them to publicly report information and interpretations that such interests might want concealed. In this way it is felt that researchers can fulfil a crucial role in an open, democratic society – that of maximizing the flow of accurate information and ideas to all interested parties in public debate.

In the context of school research, academic freedom means that researchers should be free from the constraints of politicians, education officials and school personnel which might prevent them investigating those aspects of school life they feel are important to public debate about education. They should also be free to discover the truth about these aspects of school life, and to report this to those who have an interest in knowing. Thus it is argued, for example, that researchers should not be prevented by education officials from investigating the implementation in schools of significant policy innovations, their investigations should not be constrained to produce particular findings about those innovations, and they should not be prevented from reporting their findings fully and publicly. It is suggested that this freedom, by maximizing the availability of information and ideas, will enhance the quality of public debate about policy and practice in education which is vital in a democratic society.

Having said this, I think most people (researchers included) agree that researchers' academic freedom should not be total and that researchers should not be given *carte blanche* to investigate or write anything they wish. Their conduct of research, and the publication of their findings, must clearly be bound by a commitment to discover and report the truth. As I argued in the last section, they should not be free to deliberately misrepresent the phenomena they study. Moreover, particularly where researchers are financed by public funds, their research topics must be demonstrably relevant to issues of public concern. A researcher's freedom to study absolutely anything could not be justified, although I think we should beware here of over-narrow views of relevance; sometimes research which is of little apparent or immediate relevance can be important as part of a broader, long-term programme (Hammersley, 1990a).

Most people also agree that researchers' academic freedom should be constrained by a respect for the rights and interests of research participants. It is maintained here that those who might take part in research have a right to know about research plans and the possible consequences of participation, and a right to decide whether or not to take part. It is also suggested that they have a right to privacy and to be protected from any harm that might occur as a result of the research. These ideas form the basis of three other principles which are discussed in the following sections.

INFORMED CONSENT

The idea of informed consent is that all potential participants in a research project should be able to agree or refuse to participate on the basis of full information about the research. The principle is highlighted in the various ethical guidelines, although varying degrees of commitment are expressed. The BERA (1992) guidelines, for example, are particularly emphatic. They state that honesty 'and openness should characterise the relationship between researcher, participants and institutional representatives' and that participants 'in a research study have the right to be informed about the aims, purposes and likely publication of findings involved in the research and of the potential consequences for participants, and to give their informed consent before participating in research' (p. 2).

The BSA guidelines are a little more tentative. They maintain that

'(as) far as possible sociological research should be based on the principle of freely given informed consent of those studied. This implies a responsibility on the sociologist to explain as fully as possible, and in terms meaningful to participants, what the research is about, who is undertaking and financing it, why it is being undertaken, and how it is to be disseminated'

(BSA, 1992, p. 1)

and that research 'participants should be aware of their right to refuse participation whenever and for whatever reason they wish.'

The procedure of informing participants and allowing them to refuse or consent to involvement is felt to respect their rights to know and control what happens to them and what information about them is publicly available. It is also seen as a means by which participants can protect themselves from any harm which might result from involvement. Advocates also feel that the procedure makes the value of honesty, to which all researchers should be committed, central to the research enterprise and, in doing this, informed consent is seen to protect the reputation of the research community.

The idea of informed consent suggests that all researchers who conduct observational work in schools, whether they are academic or practitioner researchers, should give comprehensive information about their research to all relevant gatekeepers and to subjects from whom data is required. As I explained in Chapter 2, in school research gatekeepers are those who are in positions of authority which enable them to control access to subjects and observational positions, and can include LEA officers, headteachers, governors, class teachers, and parents. Such people might also be subjects, but in school research subjects are often also pupils who are unlikely to be gatekeepers. It is argued that all potential participants, including pupils, should be given detailed, truthful information, in a form they can understand, about the aims and focus of the research, the questions it will address, the methodology to be adopted, and how the findings will be reported and to whom. It is also suggested that they should be appraised of the possible consequences of the research for them or for those associated with them. After receiving this information, the idea is that participants are allowed to decide freely, without coercion or undue persuasion, whether or not they wish, or wish those they are responsible for, to take part.

Sometimes research in schools takes these ideas further and encourages teachers, as research participants, to become centrally involved in the planning, conduct and reporting of the research itself. The goal of such collaborative forms of research is usually the review, evaluation and improvement of practice, and this approach eliminates, or at least blurs, the traditional distinction between researcher and teacher/subject. In such projects not only do participants decide whether or not to be involved, they also decide (or play a key role in deciding) how data is collected and used, and how the research is reported (see, for example, Simons, 1979). Interestingly, this involvement is rarely extended to pupils who generally remain subjects in the traditional sense no matter what the style of research (see Denscombe and Aubrook, 1992).

The principle of informed consent thus makes paramount commitments to openness, honesty and respect for the rights and interests of subjects. However, there are questions about whether it is desirable and practical to adopt the procedures suggested, or adopt them fully, in all research studies. One type of research where the principle is clearly not applied is in school inspection. Here, although subjects are informed about the focus and methodology of the research, they have no rights to refuse to participate or to control the information about them which is made public.[2] In school inspections the community's right to know about the quality of education provided in schools is judged to outweigh subjects' rights to exercise consent.

In other forms of research there may be circumstances where it is not desirable to give participants full information about the research. Sometimes it may be necessary to conceal the research itself, or significant aspects of the research, from all or some participants, because otherwise access to important situations will be denied, or because subjects are likely to behave differently because they know they are being observed. For example, I would imagine a researcher interested in teachers' behaviour in the staff room would be unlikely to gain access if he or she explained that this was his or her focus. And if a researcher said to teachers that he or she was interested in whether they treated boys and girls differently in the classroom I think it is highly likely that the teachers would adjust their behaviour as a result. In these situations a concealment of the researcher's identity or real purposes might be necessary in order to study teachers' usual behaviour.[3]

Milder forms of deception are also often used for the same reasons. The utilization by researchers of participant roles is based on the idea that veiling research behind such roles will encourage subjects to behave more naturally than they would have done had they been observed by a 'pure' researcher. Moreover, most researchers try to observe and record their observations unobtrusively, thereby making some effort to conceal their activities, in order to reduce reactivity.

In many situations it may also be impractical to give participants comprehensive information about the research. Accounts of research given to participants must inevitably be selective. Researchers, even when they are closely involved with participants over a long period, cannot inform them about every detail of their research, and participants may not want to know anyway. Researchers' awareness of the possible outcomes or consequences of the research may also be limited and it may therefore by difficult to alert participants to these. In ethnographic styles of research it is often the case that the focus is not completely clear at the beginning. Both topic and method are refined as the research progresses. This is one reason why the BSA guidelines (1992) suggest that 'it may be necessary for the obtaining of consent to be regarded, not as a once-and-for-all prior event, but as a process, subject to renegotiation over time' (p. 1). This may be appropriate, but a withdrawal of consent might be particularly frustrating where a researcher has already invested considerable time in his or her research. Moreover, continually drawing participants' attention to the research may disrupt the routine activities that the researcher wishes to observe, and may interfere with the development of the participant role and relationships which the researcher is trying to cultivate.

A further problem with much research in schools is that it frequently involves a large, and relatively fluid, group of participants. The main subjects of the research may, for example, be teachers but information about the children may also be important. In these circumstances it is often impractical to provide information to, and seek the consent of, all participants. And attempting to explain the research and gain the consent of new participants every time they appear on the scene would clearly be highly disruptive. There may also be considerable practical problems in schools and classrooms if some subjects are willing to give consent but others are not. It is also worth noting that informing participants about the research and negotiating to gain their consent often takes considerable amounts of time, and the greater the number of participants approached the more time is required. Inevitably resources spent in this way cannot be spent on other aspects of the research.

Another problem is that it is often difficult for the researcher to ensure that the information communicated to participants is fully grasped, and it may therefore be hard to know if they can actually make an informed judgement. This particularly applies to research with children who will sometimes not understand the researcher's aims or methods, or appreciate the possible consequences of the research. Indeed, they may have no understanding of the concept of research itself. The solution often suggested is that the researcher should seek the informed consent of important gatekeepers, such as parents or teachers acting in loco parentis, who are better able to make judgements on the children's behalf. However, even gatekeepers may not fully understand the research, and therefore not know what they are consenting (or otherwise) to. Moreover, there is sometimes a danger that gatekeepers act in their own interests rather than on their subjects' behalf.

A further question is whether it is possible for consent to ever be 'freely given'. In most cases people inevitably make decisions in the light of the views and expectations of others and few decisions are totally free of such influences. Often particularly powerful here is the influence of superordinates in institutional hierarchies. For example, a classroom teacher might find it hard to refuse a researcher access to observe his or her lessons if the headteacher made it clear that he or she thought the research was a good thing. It would probably be even more difficult for a child to refuse to participate in research if his or her teacher gave consent for the research to go ahead. Conversely, it would be very difficult for the teacher or pupil to agree to participate where the relevant gatekeeper had refused consent. Indeed, in these circumstances the researcher would rarely consult them. Researchers might strive to minimize the influence of superordinates and others, but they can never eliminate it altogether.

Another source of influence is the researcher him or herself. Researchers often try to persuade participants to give consent by using the impression management techniques I outlined in Chapter 2. They usually try to present a picture of their research as of value to participants and the community generally, and present themselves as empathetic and non-threatening. They also sometimes offer participants inducements or adopt, or take advantage of their existing, participant roles. These strategies are indicative of the tension which exists between the researcher's desire to gain access and allowing participants to 'freely' decide whether to permit it. It could be argued that some of them at least constitute 'undue persuasion'. However, some might also be seen as ways in which subjects can be more fully informed about the research and the 'real' identity of the researcher as the research progresses. For example, if the researcher plays a participant role subjects may be better able to assess his or her honesty and reliability.

A final question which should be considered is how a researcher knows whether consent has been given. Must participants actively express their consent or is the absence of a refusal, or the act of participation itself, sufficient to indicate consent? This seems to depend on the nature of the research, the type of participation which is requested and how easy it is to communicate with the individuals involved. If, for example, a researcher was seeking permission to observe a teacher's lesson for the purpose of evaluation, unless he or she was an inspector, he or she would probably need some active expression of consent. On the other hand, if a researcher wanted the permission of parents to conduct observations of children in lessons in order to discover their responses to certain curriculum materials then it might be more practical to assume consent if the parents raised no objections after receiving information about the research.

RESPECT FOR PRIVACY

Another principle which is put forward for the guidance of researchers is the idea that they should respect the privacy of the people they study.[4] This idea recognizes that there are certain physical areas and/or behaviours which participants will not want researchers to observe, or to publicly report on. There may be several reasons for this. It may be felt that observation will disturb and perhaps reduce the effectiveness of the natural social interaction which occurs in particular areas; or it may be thought that the reporting of behaviour will damage their reputation or that of others involved. More often judgements simply reflect established social conventions that certain areas or behaviours should be considered private.

Not observing, or at least not reporting, areas or behaviours participants consider private, is seen as a way of respecting their rights to decide what aspects of their lives should be open to public scrutiny and what information about them should be publicly available. Thus, the respect for privacy is closely associated with the principle of informed consent, as subjects must know the identity of the researcher and purposes of the research if they are to control access to their own privacy. Respect for privacy is also seen as a means by which participants can be protected from harm which might occur as a consequence of observation or publication. It is also felt that respecting privacy enhances the reputation of the research community.

In school research, then, the suggestion is that the views of school personnel about which areas and aspects of school life should be considered private should be sought and respected. In most schools I think there would probably be widespread agreement that areas like toilets and changing rooms, where behaviour is customarily of a private nature should be regarded as private (at least from the prying eyes of researchers).[5] In some schools a significant number of teachers (and maybe pupils) might also regard their classrooms as areas which should be private from researchers[6] on the grounds that what happens in their classrooms is their affair and also involves delicate and difficult interactions which are easily disrupted by the presence of outsiders. Many teachers might also consider the staff room an area which should be private from researchers because they think it is a place where teachers should be able to relax, express their feelings, 'let off steam', and engage in personal relationships with colleagues without fear that what they say and do will be reported publicly.[7] They might also argue that in the staff room teachers are not engaged in their professional role, and it is therefore illegitimate to scrutinize their behaviour in this context. Teachers who held such views would probably not exclude researchers from the staff room altogether, but would object to the observation of staff room behaviour for the purpose of public reporting. Many teachers and pupils might apply similar arguments to areas in school where pupils engage in peer social interaction.

Sometimes school personnel might place more emphasis on the private nature of certain behaviours or events. Staff appointment and promotion procedures, for example, are often viewed as particularly sensitive because they are centrally concerned with judgements about individual performance and merit. The conversations concerning personal relationships which occur between teachers or pupils might also be regarded as private, as might the comments teachers and pupils sometimes make about each other.

There will obviously be differing views about what parts of school life should be considered private. The important point which is suggested by this principle is that participants' views should be respected. However, as with informed consent, there are arguments that this principle should not always be paramount.

For instance, it is sometimes argued that knowledge of aspects of school life which subjects consider private may be of such public importance that subjects' views should be overridden. This argument particularly applies to the behaviour of teachers and school managers in performing their professional roles. Here it is claimed that such people (at least those in state schools) are public servants engaged in work of considerable significance, and therefore information about their behaviour is of great public importance. Indeed, it is often claimed that the public have a right to know what goes on in schools in order to judge how well public money is being spent or make informed choices about schools for their children. Such views clearly underpin recent changes in school inspections and the publication of inspection reports. Thus it is suggested that teachers have no right to claim that their classrooms or their interactions with pupils are private because their behaviour here is an important matter of public concern. Such an argument might also apply to teachers' behaviour in meetings or in the staff room. It is claimed that these too are important professional contexts. Moreover, it is suggested that teachers' behaviour in these contexts can be indicative generally of school or teacher culture which is again a matter of public concern.

Similar arguments can be applied to information about pupil behaviours that some might consider private. For example, it might be argued that information on aspects of pupils' social relationships is important in assessing the security or supportiveness of school environments, especially for more vulnerable pupils, or important in order to discover the full effects of school processes. It may be that the importance of such knowledge here outweighs any claims to privacy which are made.

Another problem is that respect for participants' views of privacy can place considerable restrictions on the strategies that researchers can use. Like the principle of informed consent, it effectively rules out deception of participants, since unless they know they are being researched and what aspects of their behaviour are the focus of attention their views about privacy cannot be elicited. It also makes the adoption of participant roles by the researcher questionable. Researchers in participant roles are often given, or have, access to arenas which subjects might consider private if they were approached by outsiders. Such researchers are able to observe situations or behaviour because they play participant roles which a non-participant would be unable to. Indeed, participant roles are advocated for precisely this reason – because they facilitate access to private areas and behaviours, and encourage subjects to avoid using public fronts to protect their usual behaviour from view. It could be argued that what is involved here is a deliberate manipulation of the researcher's identity to reduce subjects' defensiveness about privacy. As I suggested earlier, similar arguments apply to other self-presentational or persuasive techniques adopted by researchers to gain access or to reduce the reactivity their presence induces. These too might be ruled out as illegitimate attempts to manipulate subjects' views of privacy.

Such restrictions seem extreme. As we have seen there are circumstances where the deception of research participants can be justified. And the adoption of participant roles by researchers can facilitate open and productive relationships with participants in which researchers compensate them for the time and energy spent in contributing to the research, whilst at the same time gaining valuable insights into their world. There is perhaps a danger here of taking respect for privacy too far and, as a result, failing to conduct important research.

THE PROTECTION OF RESEARCH PARTICIPANTS

Another important value which is suggested should underpin research is the protection of participants from harm which might occur as a result of their involvement in the research. The various ethical codes see this as a key responsibility of researchers. For example, the BSA guidelines explain that

> Sociologists have a responsibility to ensure the physical, social and psychological well-being of participants is not adversely affected by research. They should strive to protect the rights of those they study, their interests, sensitivities and privacy, while recognizing the difficulties of balancing potentially conflicting interests.
>
> (BSA, 1992, p. 1)

And the BPS guidelines state that

Investigators have a primary responsibility to protect participants from physical and mental harm during the investigation. Normally, the risk of harm must be no greater than in ordinary life, i.e. participants should not be exposed to risks greater than or additional to those encountered in their normal life-styles.

(BPS, 1995, p. 10)

School research rarely involves a major threat to the welfare of participants, but nevertheless there are situations where participants may be harmed. Sometimes this may be the result of the research procedures. For example, if an experimental treatment involves treating some children less favourably than previously, or denying some children access to what were felt to be superior or improved resources or techniques, then their educational progress might be harmed. Similarly, if research involved taking pupils out of their normal lessons, thus taking up valuable educational time, their studies could be adversely affected. Teachers too might be affected by the stress which observation of their performance sometimes induces, especially where the perceived purpose is evaluation. Another possibility is that research participants might be harmed by the actions of researchers playing participant roles. If, for example, the researcher plays such a role ineptly both pupils and teachers might suffer. Also where researchers develop close ties with participants then they may feel emotionally let down when such ties are ended on completion of the research. Another possibility is that participants feel their trust has been violated if they find a researcher has deliberately misled them.

Probably a more serious potential source of harm is the publication of research findings or data either internally within a school or externally. Where participants can be identified and the findings or data present them in a negative light then publication may harm their reputations. For example, an account of a teacher's lessons which showed clear shortcomings might damage the status of the teacher in the eyes of his or her colleagues, with important consequences for career prospects. Even when the researcher attempts to conceal the participants' identities, it is often easy for colleagues to recognize descriptions of each other in accounts from information given about role or social position. Negative accounts may also damage the reputation of groups or institutions. For instance, a school department, or a school, or even teachers as an occupational group might be damaged by the publication of an unflattering account.

Researchers can protect participants in a number of ways. They can design the research and adopt procedures which are sensitive to the possibility of harm, and avoid the use of methods which are likely to affect participants adversely. Moreover, they can adopt, wherever possible, the principles of informed consent and respect for privacy, and so allow participants to make their own decisions about whether to take part.[8] Researchers can also avoid recording data which is likely to be sensitive, but unimportant to the research. The problem here, of course, is that it is often difficult, especially in the early stages of a research project, to know whether data is unimportant.

A more common strategy is to treat the data which is collected as confidential, storing it securely and not allowing access to it by others except in exceptional circumstances. Researchers can also do their utmost to preserve the anonymity of participants by removing direct identifying labels from data and by using pseudonyms for participants, institutions and places in both the data and publications.[9] A problem here is that sometimes institutions and participants can be recognized from the descriptions of the cases which are given in reports and data. In these situations researchers can go to greater lengths to ensure that people and places cannot be recognized. For instance, they might avoid identifying descriptions and maybe even give false information about the cases, so long as this is not centrally relevant to the report or data. Researchers might also decide to delay publication or not publish sensitive material at all. Alternatively, they can make efforts to restrict the readership of the research to certain audiences by, for example, reporting it only to those who commissioned it or only in publications with limited circulation. Finally, particularly in collaborative styles of research, they can give participants control (or at least a major say) over publication, so that they are able to decide if, when, and to whom data and findings are reported.

Whilst such strategies have usually been adopted with the protection of participants' interests in mind, it must be noted that often this is not their only purpose. Promises of confidentiality, anonymity and control over publication, for example, are also used by researchers as a means of negotiating access and encouraging participants to be more open in their behaviour. The anonymizing of participants is also used by some researchers to legitimize covert methods and invasions of privacy. The danger here is that such strategies are used rather cynically to open up situations for study, and that promises made by researchers are broken. Whilst there might be circumstances where such behaviour is justified (see below), where it is not, damage to the reputation of the research community will probably be the inevitable result.

The commitment to protect research participants is laudable, but, as with the principles of informed consent and respect for privacy, it may not be possible to achieve in all situations. Research procedures sometimes have unanticipated effects on participants which may cause them distress. And, on the publication side, once a report enters the public domain researchers have little control over what happens to it. Whilst they might make efforts to influence the interpretations and use which is made of their research, they cannot (nor should they) determine these. As a result it is possible that negative evaluations are made of participants or institutions which the researcher might not have expected and that these may have an adverse effect. Even where the identity of institutions and participants is concealed readers of research may make negative evaluations of the institutional or social categories to which they belong. More seriously, it is sometimes possible, despite the attempts of researchers at concealment, for readers to discover where the research was conducted and the identities of key participants. In these circumstances, where the report, or interpretations of it, are negative, then individuals and institutions may suffer. Of course, there is also the possibility that if reports or interpretations are positive then reputations may be enhanced. In this situation researchers may have problems preventing their research being used by participants to enhance their public image.

Protecting research participants may also not always be desirable. Clearly this is the case when the purpose of the research is public evaluation. There is always the possibility that such evaluation will be negative, and damage to the reputation of participants and/or their institution may be the inevitable and perhaps legitimate outcome of the research. This is, of course, one possible outcome of school inspections. The argument here is that parents specifically have a right to know about the quality of education in a school so that they can make informed choices for their children in the education market place. Moreover, it is claimed that the possibility, or the reality, of the publication of negative evaluations will motivate schools to improve. If this is the case, then publication may actually be beneficial rather than harmful.

Even where the goal of research is not explicitly evaluative, as I pointed out above, it can be argued that the community have a right to know about what goes on in public institutions like schools. According to this view, researchers should report what they find out about schools and should not promise schools or school personnel protection in the ways we have mentioned because they have no right to expect it. Unfortunately, few schools or teachers are committed to such openness, and certainly academic researchers are not afforded rights of access in the way that school inspectors are. The effect of such a practice would probably be to greatly restrict researchers' access to schools and classrooms.

There may, however, be circumstances where a researcher feels a commitment to report his or her findings in a form which identifies, and therefore possibly harms, either institutions or research participants, even where promises of confidentiality and anonymity have been given. This might happen if a researcher discovered what he or she felt was malpractice or some form of injustice. If, for example, he or she found systematic racial discrimination occurring in a school he or she would probably feel it was important to report it on the grounds that such practice contravened an important value principle – equal educational opportunity – to which most people in our society are committed. Indeed, such a commitment is enshrined in law, and the researcher might therefore feel bound to report the practice because not to do so would be to cover up illegal activity. Reporting such practice would obviously harm the school and key research participants, though it would hopefully help to eliminate the discrimination and thereby enhance the interests of others.

In what circumstances, when and to whom such reports should be made and whether they should or should not reveal the identity of institutions or key participants are complex and controversial questions. In my view the answers will depend on a number of factors. First, there is the question of how confident the researcher is of the accuracy of his or her description of the practice concerned. This would involve the researcher assessing the clarity of his or her definition of the concepts used to describe the practice and taking account of the potential sources of error we discussed in the last chapter. Second, there is the question of how confident he or she feels about the evaluation of the practice as undesirable. This would require clarification and justification of the value stance which might be used to judge the practice, and also consideration of other possible values and value judgements which might be significant. Third, there is the question of how serious the malpractice is in terms of the harm or potential harm to research participants or others. Also of relevance here might be how often incidents of malpractice occurred – whether they were systematic and regular or infrequent. Fourth, there is the problem of the effect of reporting on those involved. The researcher would need to judge the desirability of likely consequences, for participants and others, of different forms of reporting. Fifth, the researcher would need to think about the impact of any reporting on his or her on-going research. In reporting perceived malpractice during the research he or she might affect radically what he or she has set out to study. Moreover, his or her relationships with key participants would inevitably be affected, particularly if the intervention was seen as illegitimate, possibly resulting in the withdrawal of participants from the research. There is also the possibility that relationships with some participants could be enhanced. Finally, there is the question of how reporting will affect the reputation of the research community and therefore the prospects of future research. The researcher would have to estimate how different forms of reporting might be received by those in a position to sponsor future research.

Researchers playing participant roles often face particularly difficult problems of role conflict in these types of situation. As researchers they may feel that their duty is to protect the interests of subjects by preserving their anonymity, but as participants they may feel an obligation to report and help to eliminate any malpractice, or weakness in practice, they observe. Similarly, as researchers they may define their goal as to describe and explain in a detached way the phenomena they observe, whereas as participants they may feel the priority is to intervene to change or improve practice where they consider it necessary. If participant researchers do not report or intervene in such situations they run the risk of being accused of concealing, colluding with or even legitimizing malpractice; but if they do report or intervene they can be criticized for betraying the trust of their subjects and exceeding the boundaries of their proper influence. Which criticism is made depends how their role, or the balance between researcher and participant aspects of it, is seen by others. There is no doubt that this type of role conflict can be extremely stressful for researchers, a point which raises the issue of the effects of research on researchers themselves. (On this see Homan, 1991, pp. 166–70.)

THE PROTECTION OF THE RESEARCH COMMUNITY

Finally, it is important to briefly discuss the argument that researchers also have an obligation to protect the interests of the research community and thereby the value of knowledge production in the future. Again this value is central to the various ethical guidelines. The BPS (1995) code of conduct, for example, states that, 'psychologists shall conduct themselves in a manner that does not bring into disrepute the discipline and profession of psychology' (p. 1). And the BERA (1992) guidelines, under the heading of 'responsibility to the research profession', maintain that, 'researchers should aim to conduct their professional lives in such a way that they do not jeopardize future research, the public standing of the field, or the publication of results' (p. 2). Indeed, it can be argued that the main motivation for the development of ethical guidelines is to try to avoid the harm which can occur if researchers are seen to conduct their work in unethical ways.

Adopting practices which can be seen as unethical can damage the reputation of a particular researcher and of the institution(s) he or she represents (I include here the funders of research), but it can also harm the standing of the research community as a whole. The consequence of this may be that people's faith in research and research findings is reduced, and they are therefore less likely to co-operate with or support future research or to use its findings. This would obviously damage the interests of researchers whose careers often rest on the reputation of the professional community to which they belong. More seriously, it could mean that less research is done and therefore less knowledge is produced to inform important debates about policy and practice.

CONCLUSION

In this chapter I have discussed several key values which it is suggested should guide the conduct of researchers, and I have explored their application to observational research in schools. In considering their research questions, methods of investigation and modes of reporting researchers must make reference to these values, and decide what practices they feel are ethically appropriate for their projects. These decisions will often require them to balance competing viewpoints and interests. We have seen that the values put forward to guide research can themselves conflict. The pursuit of truth, for example, may clash with the idea that subjects have a right to exercise informed consent and have their views of privacy respected. But these values are also interpreted in different ways and given different degrees of emphasis by different parties. Decisions will therefore be difficult and controversial. Unfortunately, there are no hard and fast rules of conduct which can be applied in all situations and researchers must therefore make individual judgements related to the particular circumstances of the projects they are involved in.

NOTES

1.   For a more general and detailed discussion of ethical issues in social research see Homan, 1991.

2.   Though interestingly inspectors do not make public their evaluations of the work of individual teachers (yet!).

3.   The BSA (1992) and BPS (1995) guidelines recognize that there are circumstances where deception of subjects is justified and where it may not be possible for informed consent to be obtained. Both recommend that, if informed consent cannot be obtained before the fieldwork is conducted, wherever possible it should be obtained afterwards.

4.   There is surprisingly little explicit reference to privacy in the various published ethical guidelines. They tend to subsume discussion of it under the heading of responsibility to research participants or informed consent.

5.   It is interesting that pupils sometimes use the social convention of privacy in these contexts to conceal behaviour which is considered by teachers as deviant, and on which teachers would sometimes like information.

6.   Though it has become much more difficult in recent years for teachers to apply this to other individuals.

7.   In most schools it is an area which is clearly private from pupils and sometimes from parents or even headteachers.

8.   This strategy has been questioned on the grounds that it shifts the onus of responsibility for harm on to participants and effectively reduces the researcher's responsibility to protect them (Homan, 1991).

9.   It is important to note that anonymity may not always be in the interests of participants. Participants may find it harder to challenge a report which they believe to be false if they, or their institutions, are not named. It is possible for unscrupulous researchers to use this strategy to protect themselves or their reports from question. If this is the purpose of the use of pseudonyms then it is clearly unacceptable.

Conclusion

My aim in this book has been to describe how observational research is conducted in schools, and to discuss the issues which it raises. I have examined the various purposes of such research and how these influence the type of observational data which is collected. I have also explored how observational research is designed, the preparations that researchers make before they begin their investigations, and how observational data is recorded and analysed. In the last two chapters I have discussed the assessment of observational research and the ethical issues surrounding this type of enquiry.

This description has inevitably led me on occasions to suggest how I think research *ought* to be conducted. I am aware in my discussions of frequently drifting from description to prescription, and of often outlining ideal models of the way I think school research should be conducted. To conclude I would like to briefly summarize my views on this – on what I feel are the key characteristics of good observational research in schools.

First, I think school research should have a clear focus. In other words the aspect of school life which is the phenomenon of concern should be clearly specified. Sometimes in school research the focus may be fairly general (for example, on the nature of teaching and learning), at others a much narrower focus may be taken (for example, children's language in maths problem solving activities). More specifically, the questions which the research sets out to answer should be clear. These questions may be descriptive – the research may aim to discover the key features or characteristics of the phenomenon of concern. They may also be evaluative – the research may aim to assess the quality or effectiveness of the aspect of school life under consideration. Here it is important that the evaluative criteria or the model of good practice on which the evaluation is to be conducted are specified and justified. Sometimes questions also aim for explanation. The research may attempt to discover the causes of some phenomenon (or features of a phenomenon) or whether some aspect of school life has particular effects.

This is not to argue that the research focus or questions must necessarily be clearly established at the start of an investigation or before any fieldwork is conducted. As I have pointed out, in many school research projects the focus and questions are not clarified until the research is well under way, in fact sometimes not until data analysis begins. Nevertheless, it is important that they should be clarified at some stage.

Important too is that the focus and research questions are tailored to the resources available. There is no point in addressing questions which cannot be answered adequately given the time and physical resources at the researcher's disposal. This is an especially important consideration for practitioner researchers whose primary responsibility will be the fulfilment of their professional role, and who may therefore have very limited resources to devote to research. In general terms the less resources there are available the narrower the focus and the scope of the research must be.

A second feature of good school research is that it should have a clear and justifiable purpose. We saw in Chapter 1 that research can fulfil a variety of purposes. On the one hand, it can contribute to the development of academic empirical and theoretical knowledge about educational systems and processes. On the other, it can provide information on matters of more immediate concern to policy-makers, practitioners and others involved in education. In both cases research topics should be relevant to value concerns, and the research which is done should provide useful and valid information which goes beyond what is already known. In the former case, however, such information is likely to have a less immediate relevance than in the latter. Nevertheless the former type of research may be of great long-term significance, and we should therefore beware of over-narrow views of relevance which would confine research to the latter type.

Another characteristic of good research, in my view, is that the cases which are selected for study should be appropriate to the focus and research questions. In Chapter 2 I discussed a number of possibilities. Where information is required specifically about a particular case, as with school inspections, many studies of educational innovation, and much action research, then clearly no decision about selection of cases is required, though selection within the case will probably be necessary. Where the research questions relate to some general population – of schools, teachers, pupils, or whatever – some attempt to select a representative sample or at least a relevant cross-section of cases would be ideal. Where an in-depth picture of the phenomenon of interest is required selection may, of necessity, have to be restricted to a single case which, in some senses, is typical or illuminative. Alternatively, where research questions are explanatory in orientation, the deliberate construction of cases as in experimental designs, or the selection of theoretical or critical cases, is often needed. As I indicated in Chapter 2, similar selection strategies can be used within cases too. What is important is that researchers choose their cases carefully in order to maximize their chances of shedding light on the research questions they set themselves.

Good school research is also, in my view, characterized by methods of data collection and analysis which are appropriate to the focus and research questions. Qualitative methods, with their emphasis on flexibility, in-depth narrative accounts from an insider's perspective and the exploration of meaning, are more relevant where the aim of research is detailed description of, and exploratory theorizing about, school cultures and the social interaction occurring within them. On the other hand, quantitative methods, with their emphasis on prestructuring and accurate numerical measurement, may be more appropriate where the aims are to discover the frequency or duration of pre-specified behaviours or events or to test descriptive or explanatory hypotheses. In many research projects a combination of different methods will be necessary. In some cases qualitative and quantitative approaches may be necessary at different stages of the project; in others the different approaches may be used to explore different aspects of the phenomena under investigation.

What is also important is that methods of data collection and analysis are employed in ways which minimize the possibility of errors occurring of the type I discussed in Chapter 5. This involves taking great care with the way observations are interpreted and recorded and paying close attention to the way data are organized, stored, coded, retrieved and manipulated. It also involves researchers considering carefully the extent to which their research is affected by different forms of reactivity, and, indeed, the extent to which their own preconceptions, ideas and actions may act as a source of bias. Researchers here should adopt a consciously reflexive stance in order to assess these influences and their impact on the likely validity of their evidence and findings. Also crucial is that researchers strive to avoid procedural bias by adopting an open minded approach characterized by a willingness to utilize data from different sources, to consider different interpretations of evidence, and to actively search for evidence which might disconfirm (rather than simply reinforce) their expectations.

At a broader level, reflexivity also implies a commitment from researchers to submit their research to the scrutiny of a wider research community (see Hammersley, 1995, Chapter 4; Foster, Gomm and Hammersley, 1996, Chapter 2). To facilitate this researchers should report their research in detail, specifying clearly their findings and the evidence on which they are based. They should also describe at some length the methods that they used to collect and analyse their data, drawing attention to the limitations of their data and presenting their own assessment of the likelihood of error. As Hammersley (1995) suggests, if, on assessment, reasonably sceptical readers profess themselves unconvinced by researchers' claims, then researchers must be prepared to present further evidence, or further information about their methods, in order to clarify the basis of their findings. Such procedures will maximize the chances that the knowledge produced by educational researchers will be valid.

Finally, it is also crucial that researchers consider the ethical issues that are raised by the topics they investigate, the methods they use and the publication of their findings. Whilst I do not believe that researchers should be bound by rigid ethical rules, they should be aware of the potentially sensitive and controversial nature of their enterprise, and of the key principles which it is suggested should guide their actions. What is important is that researchers make informed and careful decisions about the ethics of their research practice which take into account the diversity of values which is relevant in particular situations.

In outlining the important features of good research practice we must not lose sight of the fact that what researchers actually do is often rather different. There are several reasons for this. Some researchers have rather different views about the nature of good research practice from those I have presented here. Perhaps more significantly, research is often a messy and disorganized business in which pragmatic considerations loom large. Moreover, time and resource constraints often mean that researchers must make uncomfortable compromises between methodological rigour and getting the research done.[1] And, of course, much research is conducted by researchers who are inexperienced and are learning their trade.

Nevertheless, there is some merit in outlining a model of good research practice. It promotes, and makes a contribution to, debates about the role and nature of educational research. It can provide guidance for new, inexperienced researchers, helping them to plan research and avoid the problems and pitfalls that can occur. Moreover, where the model, or at least elements of it, are accepted by researchers this can facilitate the development of higher standards of research practice, and, therefore, a more productive use of the resources allocated to educational research. It is in this spirit that my book is offered to readers.

NOTE

1. It is important that models of good research practice are not so ideal that they become unattainable. There are dangers of what, in another context, has been termed 'methodological purism' (Troyna, 1993, 1995) – of demanding standards of research practice which are simply too high given the constraints under which researchers operate.

References

Abraham, J. (1989) Testing Hargreaves' and Lacey's differentiation and polarisation theory in a setted comprehensive, *British Journal of Sociology*, Vol. 40, no. 1, pp. 46–81.

Abraham, J. (1995) *Divide and School: Gender and Class Dynamics in Comprehensive Education*, Falmer Press, London.

Argyris, C. and Schon, D. A. (1976) *Theory in Practice: Increasing Professional Effectiveness*, Jossey-Bass, New York.

Atkinson, M. (1984) *Our Masters' Voices: The Language and Body Language of Politics*, Routledge, London.

Ball, S. J. (1981) *Beachside Comprehensive*, Cambridge University Press.

Beynon, J. (1985) *Initial Encounters in the Secondary School*, Falmer Press, Lewes.

Bollington, R., Hopkins, D. and West, M. (1990) *An Introduction to Teacher Appraisal: A Professional Development Approach*, Cassell, London.

Boydell, D. and Jasman, A. (1983) *The Pupil and Teacher Record: A Manual for Observers*, Leicester University.

Brazil, D. C., Coultard, R. M. and Johns, C. M. (1980) *Discourse Intonation and Language Teaching*, Longman, London.

British Educational Research Association (1992) *Ethical Guidelines for Educational Research*, BERA.

British Educational Research Journal (1995) *Special Issue: Teacher Research: methodological and empowerment issues in practical research for improved teaching and learning*, Vol. 21, no. 3.

British Psychological Society (1995) *Ethical Principles for Conducting Research with Human Participants*, BPS.

British Sociological Association (1992) *Statement of Ethical Practice*, BSA.

Brophy, J. E. and Good, T. L. (1970a) Teacher–Child Dyadic Interactions: A New Method of Classroom Observation, *Journal of School Psychology*, Vol. 8, no. 2, pp. 131–8.

Brophy, J. E. and Good, T. L. (1970b) *Teacher–Student Relationships: Causes and Consequences*, Holt, Rinehart and Winston, New York.

Brown, G. A. and Wragg, E. C. (1993) *Questioning*, Routledge, London.

Bryman, A. (1988) *Quantity and Quality in Social Research*, Routledge, London.

Bryman, A. and Cramer, D. (1990) *Quantitative Data Analysis for Social Scientists*, Routledge, London.

Burgess, R. G. (1983) *Experiencing Comprehensive Education*, Methuen, London.

Burgess, R. G. (1984) *In the Field: An Introduction to Field Research*, George Allen & Unwin, London.

Campbell, D. J. and Stanley, J. C. (1963) *Experimental and Quasi-Experimental Designs for Research*, Rand McNally, Chicago.

Cavendish, S., Galton, M., Hargreaves, L. and Harlen, W. (1990) *Observing Activities*, Paul Chapman Publishing, London.

Corsaro, W. A. (1981) Entering the child's world: research strategies for field entry and data collection in a pre-school setting, in J. L. Green and C. Wallat (eds.) *Ethnography and Language in Educational Settings*, Ablex, Norwood, NJ.

Coultard, M. (1985) *An Introduction to Discourse Analysis*, Longman, London.

Cramer, D. (1994) *Introducing Statistics for Social Research*, Routledge, London.

Croll, P. (1986) *Systematic Classroom Observation*, Falmer Press, London.

Curtner-Smith, M. D., Chen, W. and Kerr, I. G. (1995) Health-related Fitness in Secondary School Physical Education: A descriptive-analytic study, *Educational Studies*, Vol. 21, no. 1, pp. 55–66.

Day, C. (1981) *Classroom-Based In-Service Teacher Education: The Development and Evaluation of a Client-Centred Model*, University of Sussex Education Area, Occasional Paper 9.

Delamont, S. (1981) All too familiar?, *Educational Analysis*, Vol. 3, no. 1, pp. 69–84.

Delamont, S. (1984) The old girl network: reflections on the field work at St.Luke's, in R. G. Burgess (ed.) *The Research Process in Educational Settings: Ten Case Studies*, Falmer Press, Lewes.

Delamont, S. and Galton, M. (1986) *Inside the Secondary Classroom*, Routledge & Kegan Paul, London.

Delamont, S. and Hamilton, D. (1984) Revisiting classroom research: a continuing cautionary tale, in S. Delamont (ed.) *Readings on Interaction in the Classroom*, Methuen, London.

Denscombe, M. and Aubrook, L. (1992) 'It's just another piece of school work': The ethics of questionnaire research on pupils in schools, *British Educational Research Journal*, Vol. 18, no. 2, pp. 113–31.

Dey, I. (1993) *Analysing Qualitative Data*, Routledge, London.

Diener, E. and Crandall, R. (1978) *Ethics in Social and Behavioural Research*, University of Chicago Press.

Edwards, A. D. and Westgate, D. P. G. (1994) *Investigating Classroom Talk*, Falmer Press, London.

Elliott, J. (1991) *Action Research for Educational Change*, Open University Press, Milton Keynes.

Festinger, L., Riecken, H. and Schachter, S. (1956) *When Prophecy Fails*, University of Minnesota Press.

Fielding, N. and Lee, R. (eds.) (1991) *Using Computers in Qualitative Research*, Sage, London.

Flanders, N. (1970) *Analysing Teacher Behaviour*, Addison Wesley, Reading, MA.

Foster, P. (1989) Policy and Practice in Multicultural and Antiracist Education: A Case Study of a Multiethnic Comprehensive school. Ph.D. Thesis, Open University.

Foster, P. (1990a) *Policy and Practice in Multicultural and Antiracist Education: A Case Study of a Multiethnic Comprehensive school*, Routledge, London.

Foster, P. (1990b) Cases not proven: An evaluation of two studies of teacher racism, *British Educational Research Journal*, Vol. 16, no. 4, pp. 335–48.

Foster, P. (1993a) Equal treatment and cultural difference in multi-ethnic schools: a critique of the teacher ethnocentrism theory, *International Studies in the Sociology of Education*, Vol. 2, no. 1, pp. 89–103.

Foster, P. (1993b) 'Methodological purism' or 'a defence against hype'? Critical readership in research in 'race' and education, *New Community*, Vol. 19, no. 3, pp. 547–52.

Foster, P., Gomm, R. and Hammersley, M. (1996) *Constructing Educational Inequality; An Assessment of Research on School Processes*, Falmer Press, London.

French, J. and French, P. (1984) Gender imbalances in the primary classroom: an interactional account, *Educational Research*, Vol. 26, no. 2, pp. 127–36.

Galton, M. (1978) *British Mirrors*, School of Education, University of Leicester.

Galton, M., Simon, B. and Croll, P. (1980) *Inside the Primary Classroom*, Routledge & Kegan Paul, London.

Galton, M. and Willcocks, J. (eds.) (1983) *Moving from the Primary Classroom*, Routledge & Kegan Paul, London.

Gillborn, D. (1990) *'Race', Ethnicity and Education*, Unwin Hyman, London.

Gillborn, D. (1995) *Racism and Antiracism in Real Schools*, Open University Press, Buckingham.

Gillborn, D. and Drew, D. (1993) The politics of research: some observations on 'methodological purity', *New Community,* Vol. 19, no. 2, pp. 354–60.

Glaser, B. G. and Strauss, A. L. (1967) *The Discovery of Grounded Theory: Strategies for Qualitative Research*, Aldine, Chicago.

Green, P. A. (1983) Teachers' influence on the self-concept of pupils of different ethnic origins. Unpublished Ph.D. Thesis, University of Durham.

Hall, V., Mackay, H. and Morgan, C. (1986) *Headteachers at Work*, Open University Press, Milton Keynes.

Hammersley, M. (1980) A Peculiar World? Teaching and Learning in an Inner City School. Unpublished Ph.D. Thesis, University of Manchester.

Hammersley, M. (1984) The researcher exposed: a natural history, in R. G. Burgess (ed.) *The Research Process in Educational Settings: Ten Case Studies*, Falmer Press, Lewes.

Hammersley, M. (1985) From ethnography to theory, *Sociology*, Vol. 19, no. 2, pp. 244–59.

Hammersley, M. (1990a) *Reading Ethnographic Research*, Longman, London.

Hammersley, M. (1990b) An assessment of two studies of gender imbalance in the classroom, *British Educational Research Journal*, Vol. 16, no. 2, pp. 125–43.

Hammersley, M. (1992) *What's Wrong with Ethnography?*, Routledge, London.

Hammersley, M. (1993) An appraisal of 'Learning to Labour', in R. Gomm and P. Woods (eds.) *Educational Research in Action*, Paul Chapman Publishing, London.

Hammersley, M. (1995) *The Politics of Social Research*, Sage, London.

Hammersley, M. and Atkinson, P. (1995) *Ethnography: Principles in Practice* (2nd edn), Routledge, London.

Hammersley, M. and Gomm, R. (1993) A response to Gillborn and Drew on 'Race', Class and School Effects, *New Community*, Vol. 19, no. 2, pp. 348–53.

Hammersley, M. and Scarth, J. (1986) The Impact of Examinations on Secondary School Teaching. Unpublished Research Report, School of Education, Open University.

Haney, C., Banks,C. and Zimbardo, P. (1973) A study of prisoners and guards in a simulated prison, *Naval Research Review*, Vol. 30, no. 9, pp. 4–17.

Hargreaves, A. (1981) Contrastive rhetoric and extremist talk: Teachers, hegemony and the educationist context, in L. Barton and S. Walker (eds.) *Schools, Teachers and Teaching*, Falmer Press, Lewes.

Hargreaves, A. (1986) *Two Cultures of Schooling: The Case of Middle Schools*, Falmer Press, London.

Hargreaves, D. H. (1967) *Social Relations in a Secondary School*, Routledge & Kegan Paul, London.

Hargreaves, D. H. (1982) *The Challenge for the Comprehensive School*, Routledge & Kegan Paul, London.

Hewitt, R. (1986) *White Talk: Black Talk*, Cambridge University Press.

Hilsum, S. and Cane, B. (1971) *The Teacher's Day*, NFER, Windsor.

Homan, R. (1991) *The Ethics of Social Research*, Longman, London.

Hopkins, D. (1985) *A Teacher's Guide to Classroom Research*, Open University Press, Milton Keynes.

Hustler, D., Cassidy, T. and Cuff, T. (1986) (eds.) *Action Research in Classrooms and Schools*, Allen & Unwin, London.

King, R. (1984) The man in the Wendy House: researching infants schools, in R. G. Burgess (ed.) *The Research Process in Educational Settings: Ten Case Studies*, Falmer Press, Lewes.

Lacey, C. (1970) *Hightown Grammar: The School as a Social System*, Manchester University Press.

Lacey, C. (1976) Problems of sociological fieldwork: a review of the methodology of 'Hightown Grammar', in M. Shipman (ed.) *The Organisation and Impact of Social Research*, Routledge & Kegan Paul, London.

Laevers, F. (1994a) The innovative project, experiential education and the definition of quality in education, in F. Laevers (ed.) *Defining and Assessing Quality in Early Childhood Education*, Studia Pedagogica, Leuven University Press.

Laevers, F. (1994b) The Leuven Involvement Scale for Young Children, LIS-YC, manual and videotape, *Experiential Education Series No. 1*, Centre for Experiential Education, Leuven.

Lambart, A. (1976) The Sisterhood, in M. Hammersley and P. Woods (eds.) *The Process of Schooling*, Routledge & Kegan Paul, London.

Marsh, P., Rosser, E. and Harre, R. (1978) *The Rules of Disorder*, Routledge & Kegan Paul, London.

McIntyre, D. and Macleod, G. (1978) The characteristics and uses of systematic classroom observation, in R. McAleese and D. Hamilton (eds.) *Understanding Classroom Life*, NFER.

McKenzie, T. L., Sallis, J. F. and Nader, P. R. (1992) SOFIT: system for observing fitness instruction time, *Journal of Teaching In Physical Education*, Vol. 11, no. 1, pp. 195–205.

Merrett, F. and Wheldall, K. (1986) Observing pupils and teachers in classrooms (OPTIC): a behavioural observation schedule for use in schools, *Educational Psychology*, Vol. 6, no. 1, pp. 57–70.

Miles, M. and Huberman, M. (1994) *Qualitative Data Analysis* (2nd edn), Sage, Thousand Oaks.

Mortimore, P., Sammons, P., Stoll, L., Lewis, D. and Ecob, R. (1988) *School Matters: The Junior Years*, Open Books, Wells.

Neill, S. (1991) *Classroom NonVerbal Communication*, Routledge, London.

Neill, S. and Caswell, C. (1993) *Body Language for Competent Teachers*, Routledge, London.

Nixon, J. (1981) (ed.) *A Teacher's Guide to Action Research*, Grant McIntyre, London.

Office for Standards In Education (OFSTED) (1993a) *Handbook for the Inspection of Schools: Framework*, HMSO, London.

Office for Standards In Education (OFSTED) (1993b) *Handbook for the Inspection of Schools: Guidance to Registered Inspectors on the Organisation of Inspections*, HMSO, London.

Office for Standards In Education (OFSTED) (1993c) *Handbook for the Inspection of Schools: Guidance on the Inspection Schedule*, HMSO, London.

Pascal, C., Bertram, A. and Ramsden, F. (1994) *Effective Early Learning Project: The Quality Evaluation and Development Process*, Worcester College of Higher Education.

Patrick, J. (1973) *A Glasgow Gang Observed*, Eyre Methuen, London.

Pellegrini, A. D. (1991) *Applied Child Study: A Developmental Approach*, Lawrence Erlbaum, Hillsdale, NJ.

Poster, C. and Poster, D. (1993) *Teacher Appraisal: Training and Implementation*, Routledge, London.

Rogers, C. (1982) *The Social Psychology of Schooling*, Routledge & Kegan Paul, London.

Rosenhan, D. L. (1982) On being sane in insane places, in M. Bulmer (ed.) *Social*

Research Ethics: An Examination of the Merits of Covert Participant Observation, Macmillan, London.

Rutter, M., Maughan, B., Mortimore, P. and Ouston, J. (1979) *Fifteen Thousand Hours: Secondary Schools and Their Effects on Children*, Open Books, London.

Sadler, D. R. (1982) Intuitive data processing as a potential source of bias in naturalistic evaluations, in E. House (ed.) *Evaluation Studies Review Annual*, 7, Sage, Beverley Hills.

Scarth, J. and Hammersley, M. (1986) Questioning ORACLE, *Educational Research*, Vol. 28, no. 3, pp. 174–84.

Schon, D. (1983) *The Reflective Practitioner*, Temple Smith, London.

Schon, D. (1987) *Educating the Reflective Practitioner*, Jossey-Bass, London.

Simon, B. and Boyer, G. (1970) *Mirrors for Behaviour, Vols. I and II*, Research for Better Schools, Inc., Philadelphia.

Simon, B. and Boyer, G. (1974) *Mirrors for Behaviour, Vol. III*, Research for Better Schools, Inc., Philadelphia.

Simons, H. (1979) Suggestions for school self-evaluation based on democratic principles, *Classroom Action Research Network Bulletin*, 3, pp. 49–55.

Simons, H. (1995) The politics and ethics of educational research in England: contemporary issues, *British Educational Research Journal*, Vol. 21, no. 4, pp. 435–49.

Singh, B. R. (1994) (ed.) *Improving Gender and Ethnic Relations: Strategies for Schools and Further Education*, Cassell, London.

Smith, D. J. and Tomlinson, S. (1989) *The School Effect: A Study of Multi-Racial Comprehensives*, Policy Studies Institute, London.

Smith, J. K. (1993) *After the Demise of Empiricism: The Problem of Judging Social and Educational Inquiry*, Ablex, Norwood, NJ.

Stenhouse, L. (1975) *An Introduction to Curriculum Research and Development*, Heinemann, London.

Stenhouse, L. (1984) Library access, library use and user education in academic sixth forms: an autobiographical account, in R. G. Burgess (ed.) *The Research Process in Educational Settings: Ten Case Studies*, Falmer Press, Lewes.

Stenhouse, L. (1985) What counts as research?, in J. Rudduck and D. Hopkins (eds.) *Research as a Basis for Teaching: Readings from the Work of Lawrence Stenhouse*, Heinemann, London.

Swann, J. and Graddol, D. (1988) Gender Inequalities in Classroom Talk, *English In Education*, Vol. 22, no. 1, pp. 48–65.

Sylva, K., Roy, C. and Painter, M. (1986) *Childwatching at Playgroup and Nursery School*, Basil Blackwell, Oxford.

Tesch, R. (1989) *Qualitative Research: Analysis Types and Software Tools*, Taylor and Francis, Philadelphia.

Tizard, B. and Hughes, M. (1984) *Young Children Learning: Talking and Thinking at Home and School*, Fontana, London.

Tizard, B. and Hughes, M. (1991) Reflections on young children learning, in G. Walford (ed.) *Doing Educational Research*, Routledge, London.

Troman, G. (1996) No entry signs: educational change and some problems encountered in negotiating entry to educational settings, *British Educational Research Journal*, Vol. 22, no. 1, pp. 71–88.

Troyna, B. (1993) Underachiever or misunderstood? A reply to Roger Gomm, *British Educational Research Journal*, Vol. 19, no. 2, pp. 67–74.

Troyna, B. (1995) Beyond reasonable doubt? Researching 'race' in educational settings, *Oxford Review of Education*, Vol. 21, no. 4, pp. 395–408.

Walford, G. (1991) Researching the City Technology College, Kinghurst, in G. Walford (ed.) *Doing Educational Research*, Routledge, London.

Walford, G. and Miller, H. (1991) *City Technology College*, Open University Press, Milton Keynes.

Webb, R. (1990) *Practitioner Research in the Primary School*, Falmer Press, London.

Wheldall, K. and Olds, P. (1987) Of sex and seating: the effects of mixed and same sex seating arrangements in junior school classrooms, *New Zealand Journal of Educational Studies*, Vol. 22, no. 1, pp. 71–85.

Whyte, J. (1986) *Girls into Science and Technology*, Routledge & Kegan Paul, London.

Willis, P. (1977) *Learning to Labour: How Working Class Kids Get Working Class Jobs*, Gower, Aldershot.

Woods, P. (1979) *The Divided School*, Routledge & Kegan Paul, London.

Wragg, E. C. (1993) *Primary Teaching Skills*, Routledge, London.

Wragg, E. C. and Brown, G. A. (1993) *Explaining*, Routledge, London.

Wright, C. (1992) *Race Relations in the Primary School*, David Fulton, London.

Index